FRIEND AND FOE ADMIT THAT NO ONE DID MORE TO INSURE THE DEFEAT OF THE AXIS THAN FRANKLIN D. ROOSEVELT.

THE REAL
F. D. R.

An intimate close-up in pictures and anecdotes, with a factual record of his life and works.

EDITED BY CLARK KINNAIRD

With an introduction by Philip S. Foner, Ph. D.

THE CITADEL PRESS • NEW YORK

LITHOGRAPHED IN THE UNITED STATES OF AMERICA BY AFFILIATED LITHOGRAPHERS, INC.

C O N T E N T S

EDITOR'S NOTE

*U*P TO NOW, more books have been written and compiled on the subject of Lincoln than there have been about any other man who ever lived, since the time of Jesus Christ, with the exception of Bonaparte. It is altogether possible that the bibliography of Franklin Delano Roosevelt will come to exceed that of both Bonaparte and Lincoln. Yet all subsequent authors and compilers of Roosevelt books must begin by consulting much the same material that was gone over in assembling this book. They must interview and read the memoirs of his intimates and antagonists; they must go through what was written about him in the contemporary press; they must study the pictures which were made of him; and they must consult and assay his speeches, his correspondence and the official records of his administration in Washington.

Those who take their view of Mr. Roosevelt at longer perspective will have an important advantage over the present-day biographer and compiler, because there is a vast amount of revelatory and significant material in records and correspondence that will not be released for publication until post-war years. Mr. Roosevelt facilitated easy access to this, when the proper time comes, by constructing a repository at Hyde Park where eventually most of it, perhaps, will be found. He had a deep sense of understanding of his place in history and the responsibility it imposed on him for keeping the record clear. Another minor piece of evidence of this, incidentally, was his habit of signing all documents and writing letters in unfading India ink. This could not be blotted; hence the multiple documents that lay scattered about him in the cottage at Warm Springs, waiting to dry, when death wrote finis to his life.

However, when all the material has been analyzed and set forth, it is unlikely that the present concept of Roosevelt will be affected much one way or the other. It will simply add bulk and controversy to future biographies.

This book was not planned as an exhaustive treatment of the subject, either pictorially or textually. It was intended not for the scholar, but for the average man, who is more interested in results than causes, in achievements than in failures. It presents the main facts of F.D.R.'s life and death; the best of the thousands of pictures of him in chronological order; the core of his philosophy which will be affecting the nation and the world for generations; and that indicator of a man's real self—anecdotes about him by his friends and by himself. While it was undertaken, frankly, in a spirit of tribute, the editor has aimed to avoid that all-too common biographical error which caused another genuinely great American, Lincoln, to write William H. Herndon:

"No, sir, I've read enough of it. It is like all the others. Biographies, as generally written, are not only misleading but false. The author of that Life of Burke makes a wonderful hero out of his subject. He magnifies his perfections, and suppresses his imperfections. He is so faithful in his zeal, and so lavish in his praise of his every act, that one is almost driven to believe that Burke never made a mistake or failure in his life. Billy, I've wondered why book publishers and merchants don't have blank biographies on their shelves, ready for an emergency; so that if a man happens to die, his heirs or his friends, if they wish to perpetuate his memory, can purchase one already written, but with blanks. These blanks they can fill up at their pleasure with rosy sentences of high-sounding praise. In most instances they commemorate a lie, and cheat posterity out of the truth."

Franklin D. Roosevelt had his mistakes and his failures. They also are here.

The editor acknowledges his indebtedness to uncounted sources for the textual material, particularly Walter Winchell, Damon Runyon, International News Service, the New York Times, the New York Journal-American, the New York Herald-Tribune, the New York Mirror, Barry Faris, George Dixon, Samuel Schulman, Robert G. Nixon, William K. Hutchinson, Seymour Berkson, Joseph V. Connolly, Inez Robb and Lee Carson.

To the student of Mr. Roosevelt's life and works, the editor commends Mrs. James Roosevelt's My Son Franklin; Karl Schriftgiesser's The Amazing Roosevelts; The Public Papers and Addresses of Franklin D. Roosevelt, collected and collated by Samuel Rosenman; Charles Michelson's The Ghost Talks; James A. Farley's Behind the Ballots; Ernest K. Lindley's The Roosevelt Revolution—First Phase; J. W. Alsop's and Turner Catledge's The 168 Days; J. W. Alsop's and R. E. Kintner's The Men Around the President; John T. Flynn's Country Squire in the White House; Compton Mackenzie's Mr. Roosevelt.

CLARK KINNAIRD.

INTRODUCTION

WHEN the news came that sunny afternoon, a hush fell over the land. Franklin Delano Roosevelt was dead! Throughout the world statesmen and humble peasants and workers joined in mourning for the architect of the coalition that was bringing victory to the forces of freedom. Everywhere people felt that someone close to them, a member of their own family, had passed away. His tragically premature death illuminated the words of Walt Whitman: ". . . there is a cement to the whole people, subtler, more underlying, than anything in written constitutions, or courts or armies—namely, the cement of a death identified thoroughly with that people, at its head, and for its sake."

It did not take death to give Franklin Delano Roosevelt his place in history: these last twelve years have left no doubt that he was among the greatest of all Americans, one who stood beside Washington, Jefferson, and Lincoln.

When the war came, President Roosevelt already had behind him a whole series of remarkable domestic reforms. By the time of his death, these sweeping changes in the body politic had come to be accepted by most Americans as permanent fixtures, foundation stones on which the better America of the future would stand.

There was an electric quality about this man, his voice and his smile, that inspired confidence. To Americans in those stormy days of economic crisis of the early Thirties, Roosevelt and his vigorous domestic program expressed hope and a vast optimism about the future. The people listened to him because he gave voice to what was in their own hearts and minds—a determination to end the senseless misery of mass unemployment. He restored their belief in American Democracy as a living, vital, growing force. They felt themselves revived by the courage and unquenchable spirit of the man who had said on assuming the highest office in the land: "The only thing we have to fear is fear itself."

Mr. Hoover turned the United States over to Franklin D. Roosevelt in 1933 with the banks closing; the economic life of the country slowing to a standstill; millions of workers unemployed, hungry, cold, evicted; hundreds of thousands of farmers unable to hold on to their land; the majority of American men and women in despair. The New Deal did more than rehabilitate an army of starving, demoralized, ragged people who had lived on relief diets for years. It did more than rebuild America's economic life and restore land to landless farmers. It did more than make it possible for an organized labor movement of less than 3,000,000 to grow to over 14,000,000. It did more than deliver historic blows against racial and religious discrimination. It did more than establish the principle that the government was responsible for the welfare and security of the people. It revived faith in America and its democratic way of life. Roosevelt proved that democracy could best be preserved through providing economic and social security for its citizens. In a Fireside Chat of 1938 he told the nation:

"Democracy has disappeared in several other great nations, not because the people of those nations disliked democracy, but because they had grown tired of unemployment and insecurity, of seeing their children hungry while they sat helpless in the face of government confusion and government weakness through lack of leadership in government. Finally, in desperation, they chose to sacrifice liberty in the hope of getting something to eat. We in America know that our democratic institutions can be preserved and made to work. But in order to preserve them we need . . . to prove that the practical operation of democratic government is equal to the task of protecting the security of the people . . ."

Better than any man of our time, Roosevelt was aware of the oneness of our world. He was convinced that the United States could not fulfill its destiny and maintain its position as "the hope of the human race," unless our people enjoyed a decent standard of living and reasonable security. He realized, too, that the world itself could not enjoy peace, prosperity and progress with a considerable section of it under the heel of fascism. He understood, therefore, that the destiny of this country was bound up so closely with that of other free and peace-loving people that we could not hope to attain full freedom for Americans unless these ideals became universal.

One of Roosevelt's first acts in the sphere of foreign policy was to announce that this country in the future would be known to our Latin-American neighbors as more than the land of Dollar Diplomacy. The "Good Neighbor" policy has paid dividends in mutual understanding. Uncle Sam, the Yankee Imperialist, has given way to the friend who realizes that inter-American problems can only be solved through courtesy and association, not by force.

Only a few months after he assumed office in 1933, President Roosevelt took steps to establish normal diplomatic relations with the Soviet Union. The importance which Roosevelt attached to this act is evident from the statement he made on October 21, 1944, in an address to the Foreign Policy Association. On this occasion he said: "I cite another early action in the field of foreign policy of which I am proud. That was the recognition in 1933 of Soviet Russia. For sixteen years before then, the American people and the Russian people had no practical means of communicating with each other. We reestablished those means. And today we are fighting with the Russians against common foes . . ."

But were it not for the first step of recognition, the grand alliance of today would have been impossible.

It took years of painful searching to build the coalition of today. During most of these years Roosevelt was in the forefront of those who pointed to the menace of fascist aggression to all freedom-loving people. Often he was ahead of the majority of the people. When, for example, in his historic Chicago speech on October 5, 1937, he demanded that the aggressor nations be quarantined, the response he met in Congress and among the people was such that he was later to write that that address "fell upon deaf ears—even hostile and resentful ears."

But Roosevelt was quite accustomed to swimming "against the current." In his early political career he had fought the Tammany machine in New York. At the Democratic Party Convention in Baltimore in 1912, he had supported the candidacy of Woodrow Wilson for President against the majority who supported Champ Clark. When others despaired of his life after he was stricken with paralysis, Roosevelt fought a successful battle for recovery.

With the background of a man who had faced and conquered supposedly insuperable obstacles, Roosevelt fought with every means in his power to educate the nation to the fundamental truth that a policy of isolationism jeopardized the national interests of the American people. To this task he dedicated himself with a fervor, a heroism, a self-sacrificing devotion that undoubtedly shortened his life. "Like most men of my age," he told the American people on accepting the nomination for a third term, "I had made plans for myself, plans for a private life of my own choice and for my own satisfaction, a life of that kind to begin in January, 1941. These plans, like so many other plans, had been made in a world which now seems as distant as another planet. Today all private plans, all private lives have been in a sense repealed by an overriding public danger. In the face of that public danger all those who can be of service to the republic have no choice but to offer themselves for service in those capacities for which they may be fitted."

President Roosevelt died before he could retire to the private life of his choice. But he lived to see the results of his program of educating the American people to the realities of the world in which we live. On the very eve of his death, Franklin Roosevelt could say with justifiable pride: "Let me assure you that my hand is the steadier for the work that is to be done, that I move more firmly into the task, knowing that you—millions and millions of you—are joined with me in the resolve to make this work endure."

Franklin Roosevelt did not live to see the day of final victory over the enemy; he did not live to see the edifice of peace to whose construction he devoted his energy, his brilliant talent and his vast experience. It is for us, the living, to complete his work by dedicating ourselves to the end that out of the agony of this war a new world will be born—the world of freedom and enduring peace for which Franklin D. Roosevelt gave his life. This, we can be sure, is how he would have had it be. "It will not be easy to create this people's peace," he told us. "But the continuance and assurance of a living peace must, in the long run, be the work of the people themselves."

Not by words alone, but only by our deeds in helping to build a United World on a basis of enduring peace and democracy can we pay a fitting tribute to the memory of our great and gallant Leader.

To this end this book is dedicated.

PHILIP S. FONER

F.D.R. IN ANECDOTE

THE stories that he himself told and which were told about him by intimates, acquaintances and unfriendly observers can mirror the personality and character of the real Franklin Delano Roosevelt better than any one biographer. Here is a representative selection of thousands of Roosevelt anecdotes:

FIRST CONTACT WITH PRESIDENCY

LONG before he himself became President, Mr. Roosevelt remembered that when he was taken to Washington first, at the age of 5, he was presented to President Cleveland at the White House. The last Democratic President before Wilson and Roosevelt expressed the wish that "you may never be President of the United States."

* * *

F.D.R. AS PROPHET

When in June, 1933, F.D.R. stopped at Eastport, Me., on his way to the family summer home at Campobello, New Brunswick, there was a reception and one speaker told this:

"When Roosevelt was paralyzed over there at Campobello [in 1921], a lot of us went to tell him good-bye on the day they took him away on a stretcher. I remember then that while he lay flat on his back he waved to us, and smiled, and said 'I'll see you again when I'm President of the United States.' "

Mr. Roosevelt grinned when the story was told, but made no comment.

* * *

WAS A BIRD OBSERVER

In addition to many other interests, F.D.R. was a lifelong ornithologist. At the age of 14, his name was already among the names of contributors to the records of bird life in Dutchess county, and observations he made of rare species are preserved in the annals of the Linnaean Society of New York. He was responsible for the recognition given by the Linnaean Society to the pioneer ornithological work in the region of Arthur Bloomfield, a butler on one of the estates.

* * *

ON HIS ANCESTRY

When a story was circulated that F.D.R. was descended from Jews, the editor of the Detroit *Jewish Chronicle* wrote the President, who replied:

"I am grateful to you for your interesting letter of March 4. I have no idea as to the source of the story which you say came from my old friend, Chase Osborn.

"All I know about the origin of the Roosevelt family in this country is that all branches bearing the name are apparently descended from Claes Martenssen Van Roosevelt, who came from Holland some time before 1648—even the year is uncertain. Where he came from in Holland I do not know nor do I know who his parents were.

"There was a family of the same name on one of the Dutch Islands, and some of the same name living in Holland as lately as thirty or forty years ago, but, frankly, I have never had either the time or the inclination to try to establish the line on the other side of the ocean before they came over here, nearly 300 years ago.

"In the dim distant past they may have been Jews or Catholics or Protestants — what I am more interested in is whether they were good citizens and believers in God—I hope they were both."

* * *

TIES WITH THE PAST

F.D.R. once told that about the age of 9 he developed a fascinated interest in Egypt — not Cairo, the Pyramids or the Valley of the Kings but the wild reaches of the Upper Nile. For years thereafter he read everything he could find on the subject, including an early book of Winston Churchill's called *The River War*, but never met any one who shared his interest.

During one of Churchill's visits, F.D.R. looked up at Hyde Park the old two-volume copy he had read as a boy and asked the author to autograph it, and discovered that he was the first person

Churchill knew who had read the book that inspired the Prime Minister's interest in the Sudan—Bruce's *Travels to the Nile*.

Many people thought that Mr. Roosevelt's political career was dedicated to kicking over traditions. But his ability to lay his hands on that book of Churchill's many years later and his careful preservation of many other things showed he was firmly attached to things in the past.

Off the front porch of the Hyde Park house is a small door, toward one end of the porch, which opens into a little room not more than twelve feet square. This is the room that was assigned to Franklin Roosevelt when he was a schoolboy. It was his lifelong private study, with books, pictures and mementos scattered helter-skelter, its furniture a collection of unrelated pieces surrounding one particularly treasured acquisition —the brass-railed desk from the old liner Washington at which President Wilson worked while going to and from the peace conference at Versailles.

*   *   *

ALMOST A SOLDIER

Soon after the enactment of the Selective Service law the President told a Broadway columnist, and permitted him to print, the story of how he almost became a U. S. Army private.

In 1898, when he was 16, he and another Groton boy decided to run away from school and join the Army in the War against Spain. That night they hid in a pie wagon which was travelling towards the recruiting station. The other boy complained of a feverish forehead.

"Mine's the same," said young Franklin, "but let's forget it. We're men now, and we have a man's job to do."

An hour later both complained of parched throats.

"Let's forget that too," said Roosevelt. "We've taken on a man's job, and we'll act like men."

But the "men" never got to the war. Both had measles.

*   *   *

A CRUSADING EDITOR

Andrew R. Kelly learned that Mr. Roosevelt shared an ambition which members of the Washington press corps undoubtedly harbored: to buy and edit a country weekly.

One night after a "command performance" in Washington of a Broadway show, the President dwelt at length on how he would run a newspaper if he had one.

F.D.R. had been a crusading editor in his undergraduate days at Harvard. As editor of the *Crimson,* he used the columns of the *Crimson* to bestir the university overseers into installing adequate fire-escapes in the dormitories. (Earlier, he had organized a relief fund for the Boers, whose republic was then being battered out of existence by the British. Even as a freshman he had called on Harvard's President Eliot and asked him if he intended to vote for McKinley and imperialism.)

But editor Roosevelt was not wholly a crusader. One coup of the *Crimson* when he presided over it was to beat Yale's collegiate daily newspaper with the story of a Harvard-Yale football game played in the Yale Bowl. Young F.D.R. arranged for a one-man handpress to be brought covertly into the Bowl. Type was set by hand during the progress of the contest, and a report of the game inserted into the first page of pre-printed copies of the *Crimson*. These were distributed within a few seconds after the final whistle, before the appearance of the *Yale News*.

*   *   *

VICTIM OF A PRANK

The President, as an old Harvard man, was once asked to authorize the use of his name on a carillon in the tower of Lowell House in a letter signed "R.P.L., secretary of the Lowell House Committee."

When F.D.R., in a letter to Prof. Julian Coolidge, master of Lowell House, said he would be greatly honored, he got a reply from Coolidge, saying there was no such person as "R.P.L." and adding: "You have been made the victim of what the French call a 'mystification,' in other words, a piece of undergraduate pleasantry."

Roosevelt replied: "I am not in the least perturbed about the chime of bells because, strictly between ourselves, I should much prefer to have a puppy dog or a baby named after me than one of those carillon effects that is never quite in tune, and that goes off at all hours of the day and night. At least one can give paregoric to a puppy or a baby.

"Very sincerely yours,

"Franklin D. Roosevelt."

*   *   *

HIS OWN ESTIMATE

In the "Thirty-fifth Annual Report" of the Harvard class of 1904, the President filled out the usual questionnaire sent to the classmen in his own handwriting. To a question concerning aversions, he replied, "None." Asked what he had written or composed, he answered, "Altogether too much."

* * *

HELPED NOMINATE WILSON

It was a little known fact that F.D.R. played a part in bringing about the nomination of Woodrow Wilson. In the Democratic Convention at Baltimore in 1912, the New York State delegation was split on the candidate. At a psychologically-important moment, young Franklin D. Roosevelt grabbed up the white, framed placard identifying the "New York" delegation, leaped into the aisle and led a parade for Wilson.

It turned the tide for the New Jersey governor and his nomination followed. Aware himself of his significance, F.D.R. preserved the placard on a wall in the room of the Hyde Park house which he used as an office.

* * *

AN F.D.R. HERO

The *New York Times* revealed that Benjamin Thompson was one of the historical characters most admired by F.D.R. Thompson is better known in history as Count Rumford—a Holy Roman Empire title bestowed after he migrated to Europe from his native Woburn, Mass. Of ample means, due to inherited wealth, he attended Harvard, experimented in science, and fought in the Revolution on the British side. In recognition of his services, the British knighted him.

After a period in England as an under secretary of state, he entered the service of the ruler of Bavaria, where he reorganized the military establishments, initiated reform in education, housing of the working-class and industry, and introduced a system of work-relief to end begging.

He reclaimed waste-land, established a farm, and used it to improve breeds of cattle. Meanwhile, he carried on experiments in the properties and utilization of heat. At his death, he left funds to establish a professorship in science at Harvard, and to endow another foundation in London.

* * *

HIS FAVORITE PASTIME

The President's last instructions to his Secretary, William D. Hassett, the afternoon he died, were to purchase the first of the new issue of the five-cent commemorative stamps to be placed on sale at the Post Office in San Francisco on the opening day of the United Nations Conference. On the trip he planned to make to the Conference he probably would have taken along stamp albums for diversion—they usually traveled with him.

One of the last subjects in the conversation he had with Mrs. Elizabeth Shoumatoff, the artist **sketching** him when he was stricken, was stamps. She asked him about the new Florida Centennial stamp and if he had any hand in the design and details of stamps in the last few years. He said he definitely did.

The President derived great pleasure from his stamps. One of the best collections extant, they numbered around 30,000. His specialties were North and South America and Hong Kong issues.

James A. Farley told how beginning in 1933, F.D.R. began to design stamps personally.

Mr. Farley, then Postmaster-General, recalled how one day F.D.R. sat in his office for an hour sketching out designs for new stamps to be issued in connection with Rear Admiral Richard E. Byrd's expedition to the South Pole.

"The thing that impressed me most," Farley said, "was the fact that with the entire country whipped up to a fever of excitement over the NRA, the AAA, and the other policies of the new administration then being put into effect, the President was able to put all those things out of his mind while he sat working at his hobby."

Farley revealed that F.D.R. was responsible for the famous "Mother's Day" stamp, the design for which he drew in February of 1934, taking Whistler's portrait of his mother as a model. Farley recalled F.D.R. drew that one sitting in bed. He has the sketch, which is about five and one-half inches long and three inches deep.

The Mother's Day stamp was initiated by a private organization. The Post Office Department is constantly beset with requests for such special issues. Farley used to take them over to F.D.R. for decision. He recalled, "One fellow, evidently an anti-New Dealer, wrote in suggesting a stamp commemorating the Supreme Court's decision overturning the NRA. I slipped this one in along with the rest and said nothing. The President came across it, chuckled, and said, 'All right. I'll draw you a picture of a sick chicken.' "

His mother, Mrs. James Roosevelt, in her book, *My Son, Franklin Delano Roosevelt*, says as a little boy he shared the hobby of stamp collecting with other little boys. His father started him at it.

"As time went on, he acquired a remarkable slant on geography. This he attributed largely to his interest in stamp collecting."

The President also took upon himself the designing of our coins. At the time half-cent and one-mill coins were proposed in 1936, to facilitate sales taxes, F.D.R. talked to Treasury Secretary Morgenthau about them, and sketched what they should look like. The one-mill coin was to be square; the half-cent piece was to have a hole in it. Morgenthau ordered the designs to be followed, but they were not used because issuance of the coins was abandoned.

Mr. Roosevelt also chose to name all new naval vessels, working from long lists of possible names prepared by Navy experts. It was fitting that one of the biggest aircraft carriers was given his name soon after his death.

*   *   *

EXPERT ON GEOGRAPHY

On the President's trip to the Casablanca conference in 1943, he paused in Liberia to inspect American forces there, and dust whirled up by the procession of jeeps bearing the official party, made the faces of the Presidential group as brown as a walnut. The President enjoyed himself immensely kidding his companions about being so dirty.

In flying across the Atlantic, on this trip, the President's great knowledge of geography was shown by the fact that he beat the pilot and navigator to it in pointing out the headlands—he navigated the ship in passing over Haiti.

*   *   *

A LINCOLN PARALLEL

At his first press conference after his return from his "Atlantic Charter" meeting with Winston Churchill, in August, 1941, he was asked questions which he countered with a long quotation from Lincoln. Mindful that on past occasions Mr. Roosevelt had sometimes jocularly suggested to his interviewers how the "lead" on the story should be written, a reporter inquired:

"Mr. President, if you were writing the lead for this story, what would you say?"

F.D.R. provided a headline, "President Quotes Lincoln and Draws Parallel," that many newspapers used.

The quotation was an excerpt from Mrs. Mary A. Livermore's conversation with Lincoln in 1862, as recorded in Carl Sandburg's biography of the Civil War President, concluding, "They (the people) have no idea that the war is to be carried on and put through by hard, tough fighting, that it will hurt somebody; and no headway is going to be made while this delusion lasts."

It was a rather interesting parallel, President Roosevelt said, referring specifically to Lincoln's belief that this country had not awakened to the fact that we had a war, although it had been going on for a year.

This was three months before Pearl Harbor.

*   *   *

A LINCOLNESQUE STORY

There were many parallels in the characters and histories of Presidents Lincoln and F.D.R., hence it is not strange that there is a similarity between many Lincoln and F.D.R. anecdotes. There is, for example, the story earlier told about Lincoln, and later attributed to Mr. Roosevelt, inspired by quarrels between Northern and Southern Democrats.

The President said he knew a man named Jones, a devout churchman, who was a member of an equally religious group of highway commissioners, having supervision of the erection of a bridge over a swift and dangerous river. Several engineers had been consulted who had made cost estimates out of all proportion to what the commissioners felt should be spent. Jones induced the commission to call in his friend Smith. "Can you build this bridge?" inquired the commissioners. "Yes," replied Smith. "I could build a bridge to Hell, if necessary."

One or two commissioners were evidently shocked at this impious language, and Jones felt called upon to defend his friend. "I know Smith so well," said he, "and he is so honest a man, that if he states positively that he can build a bridge to—to—the infernal regions, why I believe it; but I feel bound to say that I have my doubts about the abutment on the other side."

"So," said the President, "when politicians tell me the northern and the southern wings of the party can be harmonized, I believe them, of course, but I have my doubts about the abutment on the other side."

*   *   *

ON CABINET CHANGES

F.D.R. was sometimes subjected to criticism because of his evident reluctance to replace members of his Cabinet who, the critics thought, had outworn their usefulness. He recalled a story President Lincoln told some gentlemen who, after Secretary of War Simon Cameron had already been "persuaded" to resign, still pressed for other changes to be made:

Joe Wilson built himself a cabin down in the river bottoms and started a flock of poultry. At length he got together a choice lot of young fowls, but began to be the victim of depredations of those little black and white-spotted animals which it is not necessary to name. One night Joe was awakened by an unusual fluttering among his chickens, and grabbing his old musket, crept out. He sighted a half dozen of the pests running in and out of the shed laden with loot. Joe let go with his musket and tried to clean out the whole tribe. He killed only one, the others scampered away. In telling the story, Joe would pause here and hold his nose.

"Why didn't you follow them up and kill the rest?" inquired the neighbors.

"Blast it," said Joe, "it was eleven weeks before I got over killing one."

* * *

A MODERN PARABLE

At another time when his advocacy of business reforms was being fought, it is said the President recalled a Lincolnesque story about an armed ruffian who made an unprovoked assault in a highway upon a citizen. The latter, instead of acquiescing, made a spring and wrested the weapon from the ruffian. "Stop," said the latter, "give me back that pistol, you have no right to my property."

* * *

A BIBLICAL POINT

There is a legend that in early days of his administration, a follower of the President sought to get him to accept a certain group of financial men as his advisers in the preparation of a fiscal move, saying, "I can vouch for their patriotism and loyalty; for as the good book says, 'Where the treasure is, there will be the heart also.'"

To which came the answer: "There is another text that might equally apply: 'Where the carcass is, there will the eagles be gathered together.'"

* * *

CONGRESSIONAL REJOINDER

A member of Congress who was an old friend and had the privilege of speaking his mind, heatedly declared to the President at the White House one day, "This administration is on the way to hell—it's not a mile away from it this minute!"

The President chuckled and replied, "That's the exact distance from here to the Capitol."

ON UNDERSTANDING MEN

F.D.R. once was moved to say, "A columnist complained the other day that I had overestimated the importance of understanding of, and sympathy with, the point of view and the general well-being of what might be called the average citizen, and he intimated that a man could be highly successful in any profession without studying that point of view.

"Nevertheless, when you make a close examination of any profession, you will find very few successful men, or, for that matter, women, who do not take into consideration the effect of their individual efforts on humanity as a whole."

* * *

AS UNCLE JED SAID

A visitor reported having heard F.D.R., in commenting on some of his critics, tell this story about an old town character, Uncle Jed:

"Uncle Jed," said Ben, one day, "ain't you gittin' a leetle hard of hearin'?"

"Yep," said Uncle Jed, "I'm afeerd I'm gittin' a mite deef."

Whereupon Ben made Uncle Jed go down to New York, to see an ear doctor.

Uncle Jed came back. And Ben asked what happened. "Well," said Uncle Jed, "that doctor asked me if I had been drinkin' any. And I said 'Yes, I been drinkin' a mite.'

"And then that doctor said, 'Well, Jed, I might just as well tell you now that if you don't want to lose your hearin' you've got to give up drinkin'.'

"Well," said Uncle Jed, "I thought it over; and then I said, 'Doc, I like what I've been drinkin' so much better than what I've been a-hearin' that I reckon I'll jest keep on gittin' deef!'"

* * *

TIME FOR NEUTRALITY

When some political feudists within the party sought to get the President to intervene, he was quoted as replying, "I learned a great many years ago that in a fight between a man and his wife, a third person should never get between the woman's rolling-pin and the man's boot."

* * *

HE KNEW BY EXPERIENCE

A White House visitor asked him, "Mr. President, how in the world did you acquire such patience—with all the bores you meet in a day?"

F.D.R. replied: "You acquire patience after you've spent two years learning how to wiggle your big toe again."

ONE OF HIS OWN STORIES

Once, apropos some criticism, F.D.R. told this story:

"After the First Battle of the Marne, in the World War, most thought that it was Marshal Joffre who had won it, but some refused to agree.

"One day, a newspaperman appealed to Marshal Joffre: 'Will you tell me who did win the Battle of the Marne?'

"'I can't answer that,' said the Marshal. 'But I can tell you that if the Battle of the Marne had been lost the blame would have been on me.'"

*   *   *

BOOK VS. MOTHER KNOWLEDGE

The President related, "Somebody told me a story of an old Negro who once said: 'He got a lot of book knowledge but he ain't got no mother knowledge.' There is a lot in that, it is not book knowledge alone that counts most."

*   *   *

TURNING THE TABLES

When, through error, a number of Republicans received the form letter with which sponsors of a Jackson Day Dinner in Washington solicited reservations at $100 a plate, news services carried the story, and a Republican county committee in Illinois invited President Roosevelt to buy a couple of tickets to its dinner hailing a local Republican politico. The President laughed and bought a couple of tickets, the price of which was 50 cents, for himself and his secretary, Steve Early.

*   *   *

A FRANKFURTER ADDICT

F.D.R. loved hot dogs as Wimpy loves hamburgers. More than once on motor trips, the Presidential automobile stopped at a roadside stand to permit the Chief Executive to enjoy a couple of hot dogs "with plenty of mustard" washed down with a glass of draught beer, as he sat in the car. When Mrs. Roosevelt accompanied him, she was likely to have one frankfurter sandwich for herself, accompanied by ice water. F.D.R. introduced King George and Queen Elizabeth to hot dogs when the British sovereigns visited Hyde Park.

*   *   *

A BASEBALL FAN

The President genuinely liked baseball. When at Hyde Park he sometimes motored over to see soft-ball games organized by Lowell Thomas and other well-known Dutchess county residents. Once the President managed a team which challenged a nine gotten together by Thomas. When Rexford Guy Tugwell, pitcher for the President's team was hit freely, FDR yanked him out with evident delight.

Caswell Adams recalls that while President, F.D.R. said: "When it comes to baseball I am the kind of fan who wants to get plenty of action for his money. I have some appreciation of a game which is featured by a pitcher's duel and results in a score of one to nothing. But I must confess that I get the biggest kick out of the biggest score —a game in which the batters pole the ball into the far corners of the field, the outfielders scramble, and men run the bases. In short, my idea of the best game is one that gaurantees the fans a combined score of not less than 15 runs, divided about eight to seven."

*   *   *

LEARNED TRICKS OF PHOTOGRAPHY

Sammy Schulman of INP, tells a story illustrative of the President's warm-hearted consideration for old friends. Sammy, sent to Casablanca for an assignment undisclosed in advance, suddenly discovered he was covering a meeting of Churchill and Roosevelt:

"About noon he was driven into a field where a mess had been set up and sat down at one of the small wooden tables that had been placed in the open. Generals Clark and Patton and Harry Hopkins sat down with him on the folding chairs and shared a lunch of ham and mashed potatoes with fruit salad and coffee, which the President ate heartily.

"When he had finished he looked around a moment and said, 'Where's Sammy?' I heard him and got up from my table not far away. When he saw me he wagged a finger and I went over and shook hands with him.

"'How are you standing up under the punishment?' he ask me. I told him okay, and then he told me that he had heard that I had been of help at Fedala on the morning of the invasion. I told him that it was a pleasure, which it was. He talked then about the men he had seen, the fighting men, and the condition they were in. He showed in a few sentences how much he knew about the country, and he said he was very pleased with the way in which the North African operation had worked thus far.

"Churchill said later it was Roosevelt who had planned the African invasion.

"I've never known anybody who could drop from a really lofty line of thinking and swoop down to the smaller things of life more easily than the President can. In the middle of his comment on the enormity of the whole North African occupation he'd ask me some little personal question that showed how he remembered things.

"At the end of the mass interview with the press he arranged during the conference, the President said, 'Now, gentlemen, I'd like to meet all of you, and so would Mr. Churchill.' There were about thirty of us. We formed a line and introduced ourselves to the President who in turn introduced us to Churchill. When it came my turn the President let out a laugh and, while he was shaking hands with me he turned to Churchill and said:

" 'And this is Sammy.'

"Churchill took the cigar out of his mouth and said, 'Oh?'

"The President explained to him that we had been on a lot of trips together, that I had a record for missing trains, and that once he had had to order a train stopped because he saw me running down a station platform trying to catch it.

"I guess maybe he remembered the time when right after his nomination the first time, he decided he'd better know more about picture-making. On the way from New York to Columbus, where he was to make one of his first stump speeches, I was sitting in a card game in the newspapermens' car when he sent word that he wanted to see me. I followed the messenger back to his private car, wondering what was up.

"He was busy with something else when I came in, but after a moment he looked up, smiled and invited me to sit down. Then he ordered a sandwich for me, and, of all things, a bottle of ale. That was prohibition days and people like me practically never saw ale.

"When he had finished what he was doing he said, 'Now . . . There are some things I don't understand about your business. I want to know everything about it.' And he began asking me the darnedest variety of questions about photography. He wanted to know why certain poses were better than others; why so many shots were made of the same subject under identical circumstances; how the stuff was developed; how the pictures were serviced to clients; what kind of cameras I used; what kind of film; a list of our standard difficulties and how they might be remedied—everything. Satisfied at last, he thanked me and went back to work."

SAMMY PICTURES F.D.R. AT CASABLANCA

A DESERVING DEMOCRAT

The day Harry Hopkins was to be appointed Lend-Lease boss, Walter Winchell reported, some of his critics among the White House press asked F.D.R. to define his job. Because some annoyed him (because they thought he was evasive), F.D.R. just didn't say anything — he merely sphinxed.

"Will you please tell us his position?" persisted one reporter.

"He will be an administrative assistant," parried F.D.R.

"Will he be paid?" sassed another scribe.

The President wiped his specs, squinted up at the boys and purred: "Sure. He's a Democrat, isn't he?"

* * *

A POINT OF DIFFERENCE

Lieut. Jim Rowe, one of F.D.R.'s favorites, frequently took on the President in vigorous argument, Walter Winchell recalls. On one issue in which they were in violent disagreement, Jim repeatedly attacked the Presidential view. Summing up what he thought were the merits of the question, Rowe said: "And I think, Mr. President, I have marshaled every relevant factor in this situation."

"No, you haven't, Jim," said F.D.R. very gently. "By some strange oversight, the American people elected me President and not you."

* * *

FIRST AID TO THE TONGUE-TIED

President Roosevelt used to astound some lesser known White House first-time visitors by his seeming familiarity with all their doings.

"That man must know everything!" was a common reaction. "He not only knew I made my money in the plumbing supply game but you'd think he'd been in it himself. He talked to me about vent caps, backwater valves, cleanout screws and flushometers like a master plumber."

George Dixon wrote that Mrs. Roosevelt used to provide a lot of the data with which the President put the visitors at their ease.

"Mrs. Roosevelt, of course, had research assistance from the White House secretariat, but she usually took it upon herself to whip it into final shape. This was her private labor of love; the contribution of the loyal helpmeet.

"This advance dope proved particularly effective at formal White House dinner parties. Before going in to dinner, Mrs. Roosevelt handed her husband a card identifying various guests and including a quick resume of things they were interested in.

"The result was that Mr. Roosevelt could take a glance at the card under cover of his napkin and then say to a guest he had just seen for the first time:

" 'And how's everything in Upper Darby, Mr. Pillsbury? I hear you've been doing great things with your non-potable brake mixture!'

"Well, that was all the President had to say because the fellow—practically exploding from the sudden realization of his own importance—would carry the conversational ball from then on."

Other hosts and hostesses in Washington caught on and adopted the idea when they had unfamiliar guests, but usually with less finesse, and sometimes with amusing results.

*   *   *

THANKS TO WINCHELL

Walter Winchell once saw him weep.

"It happened when ex-Congressman Lambertson and others were criticizing the war records of his sons," Winchell wrote after the President's death. "Mr. Roosevelt was miserable about a letter that came (that morning) from one of them. It concluded: 'Pop, sometimes I really hope one of us gets killed so that maybe they'll stop picking on the rest of the family!'

"When he read it, F.D.R.'s lower lip started to quiver, and the tears came. I turned away and swallowed hard.

" 'Will you please let me tell that Sunday night?'

" 'No, you mustn't,' he said, and changed the subject.

"I wrote to Mrs. Roosevelt about it. 'Won't you please,' said the note, 'get the President to release me from that pledge not to make it public? The people should know these things. . . . I happen to know that Elliott was almost lost rescuing others in the far North. I know too, that Frank was nearly swept overboard at sea, helping a sailor!'

"Mrs. Roosevelt's note was short: 'If he told you not to print it, don't do it.'

"But Lambertson wouldn't stop. He made a daily accusation in Congress. I made it public and evened up matters once and for all with Mr. Lambertson (since defeated) by announcing exclusively: 'Congressman Lambertson, who keeps denouncing the war records of the Roosevelt boys—himself is the father of a son—who yesterday applied for deferment in the draft—on the ground that he is a conscientious objector!' "

"F.D.R.'s lovely Girl Friday (Grace Tully) phoned.

" 'That was some little trick you performed last night,' she said.

" 'You mean I'm in the pup tent?' I fished.

" 'Better get down here today,' said Miss Tully.

"In his office the front pages confirming the Lambertson lad's 'conscientious objector' yarn were on his desk.

"The President tapped the article with his cigarette holder—smacked his lips—and said: 'thanks.' "

*   *   *

HIS UNLUCKY SUIT

Winchell also is the source of the story that back in 1940, a Republican senator was teasing F.D.R. about his "lucky inaugural suit." "If you run for a third term," heckled the senator, "let

F.D.R. AND VICE PRESIDENT GARNER EXCHANGE SOME STORIES AT JACKSON DAY DINNER IN 1940

me borrow that suit, and I'll run against you and win!"

F.D.R. told him he couldn't let him borrow his lucky suit, "Because I may need it myself!"

"You mean," was the retort, "that you *are* going to run again?"

"I mean," said Mr. Roosevelt, "that I may need it myself. I do not consider it my inaugural suit. It is my—funeral suit."

Once he spoke with a grimace of 60 as "the dark age."

* * *

JAMES' FOREBODING

In 1940, when demands rose within the party for him to run for a third term, James Roosevelt was on the White House staff and was called in when the President asked his advisors to confer with him and submit reasons why he should run. When the conference was over, Jimmy said: "Are you trying to kill my father? No man can live through three terms in that job."

"Jimmy," said a conferee, "he's your father, but he belongs to the world!"

There is other evidence that members of the family did not expect or want F.D.R. to submit to more than eight years of the Presidency.

* * *

NOT ALWAYS RIGHT

When F.D.R. was asked in a press conference in October, 1944, if he had figured out the winner of the election, he replied he had. This got a good laugh. To which he quipped: "I might add that I have not always been right!"

* * *

NO JOBS FOR SALE

In his *The Ghost Talks,* one of the best and most dispassionate commentaries on the Roosevelt regime, Charles Michelson told of the time an eminent businessman called on him and offered to produce $200,000 for the Democratic National Committee's campaign fund.

Michelson mentioned it to the President in the course of a conversation.

"You know," F.D.R. said, "that that gentleman is a candidate for a high diplomatic position?"

"I believe he is."

"Well, you know he is not going to be appointed to that place?"

"I know it now."

"If the committee took that money he would have a right to assume that he had bought something; so you will have to get along without it."

"POORER BUT WISER"

"I am a poorer and a wiser man now than I was when I went to Albany as Governor in 1928," was his only comment, given with a chuckle, when during the 1940 campaign Wendell L. Willkie suggested that Presidents as well as other elective officials be required to file statements of assets on entering and leaving office.

* * *

A BUSY MAN

When Mr. Roosevelt was governor of New York, he got to know a film salesman named Moe Schenck, who worked out of Albany.

One day Moe was in the White House Executive offices to see Steve Early about a picture he was representing. He emerged from Early's office just as F.D.R. was coming down the corridor.

With his accustomed heartiness on seeing old acquaintances F.D.R. cried out:

"Why, Moe, you old son of a gun! What are you doing here?"

Moe, who takes life very seriously, explained his mission.

"Well, good luck, Moe," rumbled F.D.R. "But don't make yourself a stranger. Why don't you come in and see me now and then?"

"Mr. President," said Moe, "I'm a very busy man."

* * *

PREPARING SPEECHES

Literally scores of men were credited at one time or another with being "ghost-writers" for F.D.R. Mr. Michelson, who was among them, provides in his valuable book a picture of the preparation of an F.D.R. speech.

Hugh Johnson, Raymond Moley and Michelson were summoned to the Roosevelt home to draft a speech to be delivered at Columbus, O. Each brought a manuscript with him. Johnson's product bristled with fulminations of Johnsonesque calibre. Moley presented the economic and social issues. Michelson set forth straight politics with some covert digs and sly insinuations at the Republicans. None of the three speeches was delivered. Instead F.D.R. suggested each topic, and the three went to typewriters and ground out their views of the proper presentation. Then after a brief discussion of these, F.D.R. stretched himself on a couch and with his eyes on the ceiling dictated his own version, occasionally using one of the trio's phrases but generally putting things in his own way.

"So far as I know, this was the practice with every speech," Michelson said. "Franklin Roosevelt was a better phrase-maker than anybody he ever had around him."

*   *   *

LOVED PEANUTS

A peanut vendor, an immigrant from Greece, learned that *no one* was beneath the notice of the President of the United States. His peanut-stand was at the curb of a street bordering the White House and eventually local officials decided it was a nuisance and sought to evict him. The President made an appeal for him and the peanut vendor kept his stand.

F.D.R. had a typical American's taste for peanuts. Once, during a particularly busy time at the White House, Robert Sherwood and another of the President's speech-writing assistants were working there when they reached an impasse and asked to see the President. "We need about 20 minutes," they told Grace Tully, his stenographer.

"You may see him, but only for five minutes," she told them.

"But we really need 20 minutes," they insisted.

Miss Tully was adamant: *"Five* minutes!"

While they were waiting for an appointment, another White House aide whispered: "Get a bag of peanuts."

Sherwood went outside to get peanuts and when he was ushered into the President's office for the five minute talk, F.D.R. noticed the large paper bag he bore and said, "What've you got there, Bob?"

Sherwood told him they were peanuts. They munched them for 40 minutes.

*   *   *

ESCAPING PUBLIC NOTICE

It was the President himself who "let the cat out of the bag" and told with delight the trickery the Secret Service had resorted to to divert attention from him during his travels in Africa. One trick was for a Secret Service man to pretend to fall out of a jeep, his companions grabbing and hauling him back in. The device that was the President's favorite, it was evident, was that of two Secret Service operatives who rode ahead of his car and when they saw a European, would point excitedly to the sky and exclaim, "Look! Look!" While the European hunted the sky overhead, the President rode by unnoticed.

SUGGESTION TO A BIOGRAPHER

When Emil Ludwig began work on the biography of Mr. Roosevelt, commissioned by an American publisher, he said: "this is a new and difficult job for me, Mr. President. My biographies of Napoleon, Bismarck, Goethe and Bolivar were much easier to write. It is hard to appraise you, because you are still living."

The President clutched the biographer's hand, and interrupted Ludwig's note-scribbling. "In that case," F.D.R. laughed, "I have a suggestion to make—let's both wait one century."

*   *   *

FLIGHT OF FANCY

Walter Winchell wrote that when the two met in Quebec Mr. Churchill is supposed to have asked F.D.R. why Americans believed obviously false statements made by his foes.

"You know," added Churchill, "such rumors haven't a leg to stand on."

"It's like the old Chinese proverb," said the President. "A lie has no legs and cannot stand, but it has wings and can fly."

*   *   *

NO DRINKER

Wherever Mr. Roosevelt sojourned in later years, he took his own bottled water with him.

At the Teheran Conference one day, George Dixon revealed, Winston Churchill wasn't feeling so good and F.D.R. suggested it might be the water. He offered some of his supply, but Britannia's Prime Minister declined abruptly.

"You know very well," Churchill said in hurt and reproving tones, "that I never drink water!"

*   *   *

ONE ERROR HE LIKED

Upon the occasion of one of his illnesses, a Washington newspaper ran a story headlined: "F.D.R. Kept In Bed With Slight Coed." He howled over the typographical error, and sent out for several copies.

*   *   *

A COLD REMEDY

When he campaigned in a heavy rain in New York City in 1944, it was necessary for his physician to prescribe some brandy and tea for him at the end of a long auto ride.

"Don't forget, Mr. President," he was told, "you have a speech to deliver tonight."

"Yes," said F.D.R., winking, "and the subject is not prohibition."

PRESIDENT AND MRS. F.D.R. RIDING IN THE RAIN IN AN OPEN CAR, ON HIS SECOND INAUGURATION DAY.

HE COULD TAKE IT

When inclement weather caused it to be suggested that the 1937 inauguration be held indoors, F.D.R. referred to the crowds that were waiting outdoors and said, "If they can take it, I can."

PERILS OF POLITICS

An old New York State friend is supposed to have come to the President, on one of his gray days, to ask his advice about running for sheriff.

"Don't do it," warned the President, "You'll no sooner get the position than they will be accusing you of graft or something."

The visitor didn't take the President's advice. The President saw him some months later and chided him: "I see you got the office. Now I suppose they are accusing you of graft."

The man laughed, "Accusing me! Why, they've proved it on me!"

ONE PLAN FOR FUTURE

Some months before his death, Mr. Roosevelt told an old Hyde Park friend, "My greatest desire is to come back to Hyde Park and settle down to grow trees."

To reporters who accompanied him on one of his trips to Hyde Park he once spent several hours showing his forest projects there and explaining how after a continuous planting project he had begun, was ten years old, he could expect to profit $40 an acre a year from the wood crop.

A SOUND SLEEPER

F.D.R. was one man who never claimed he couldn't sleep on a train. He boasted that he slept better on a pullman; and once orders were given to stretch out a run to give the President more sleep.

NO REBUKE

New York's Mayor LaGuardia told of President Roosevelt's reaction when in 1939, LaGuardia declared publicly that Adolf Hitler should be exhibited in a "chamber of horrors."

"I called at the White House soon afterward to keep an appointment made before I made the remark," the mayor said. "The press and many persons thought I went there to be reprimanded because the German ambassador had lodged a protest on behalf of his government.

"The President smiled as I entered his office. Then he extended his right arm and said, 'Heil, Fiorello!' I snapped to attention, extended my right arm and replied, 'Heil, Franklin!' And that's all that was ever said about it. Incidentally, it was the only time I ever addressed the President as Franklin. I always called him 'Chief' or 'Mr. Roosevelt.' "

A MOVIE FAN

President Roosevelt was an ardent movie fan. His office staff would call up the exchanges and, in the projection room on the second floor, they would run the latest features for him. He got a kick out of having Lana Turner seated next to him at a luncheon. When he went off on a trip he always saw that the cruiser he traveled on was supplied with the latest pictures.

CURTAILING CALLS

F.D.R. was so prone to upset his schedule of official appointments if he got into an interesting conversation with a visitor or the visitor gave him a lot of laughs, that his secretaries sometimes had to conspire against long calls. When there was a pressing schedule to be fulfilled, and there were groups of visitors due who might begin a "story bee," they removed the chairs for visitors from his office.

* * *

FOR SOUVENIR HUNTERS

Because so many of his visitors carried off White House matchbooks as souvenirs, F.D.R. puckishly had them imprinted "Stolen from the White House."

* * *

A GOOD REASON

Asked why he aspired to be President in a crisis, his answer was: "Some one has to!"

* * *

NEVER A PESSIMIST

Mrs. Roosevelt once said, "I have never seen Franklin discouraged."

* * *

TIME WAS UP

Walter Winchell told of the time F.D.R. was in one of his windy moods, and the crowd of reporters in the Oval Room shifted restlessly because of the sweltering humidity. A Chicago scribe noticed the President was uncomfortable, too. He called out the signal that breaks up press conferences in the White House: "Thank you, Mr. President." But one man, who enjoyed heckling F.D.R., yelled for another query.

"Didn't you just hear, 'Thank you, Mr. President'?" said F.D.R.

"I didn't hear him say it," said the heckler.

"Well, I heard him say it," shouted F.D.R., and the mob howled.

* * *

DOCUMENTED FISH STORIES

Fishing was Mr. Roosevelt's principal outdoor hobby. He fished nearly every sea in the Western hemisphere, in motor whalers and swivel-chaired launches, in schooners and from the Presidential yacht.

No one could take F.D.R.'s fish stories lightly. During a cruise on Vincent Astor's yacht *Nourmahal*, when the absent correspondents were dependent on daily bulletins from aboard and interviews with visitors to the yacht for news of the Chief Executive's doings, Elliott Roosevelt returned from a stay with his father and told reporters his father had spent a luckless fishing day in the tropical waters of the Bahamas, implying that was usual. When the statement got into print, the President called the reporters to the yacht for an "investigation" to determine whether Elliott was guilty of "gross libel."

The President called upon one member of the fishing party, Judge Frederick Kernochan, to preside and summoned all others aboard as witnesses, announcing they had "waived immunity." The witnesses then swore that the President caught with his own hands groupers, marlins and fighting barracudas, and gave testimony regarding the President's hooking of his favorite fish, the fighting bone-fish, by trolling (which old salts said was impossible).

On a later fishing trip, he offered physical evidence of his fishing ability, by sending a 100-pound turtle over to an escorting destroyer to provide toothsome steaks for the crew.

* * *

LAUGHS ON HIMSELF

The President would turn the laugh on himself. In a conversation with a group of New York Liberal Party leaders on a day that a U. S. fleet won a major Pacific battle, he remarked that there was a world wide sweep of liberalism and the U. S., as usual, was leading the way. He recalled that way back in 1848, a U. S. warship in the Mediterranean had provided a safe haven for a Hungarian radical fleeing from the Austro-Hungarian emperor's police. "That was in the administration of," he went on, then paused, "say, who was President then?"

One of the visitors remarked it was difficult to recall the name of any other President and F.D.R. laughed heartily.

Another earlier time, when he was at issue with Congress over an appropriation measure, the President cracked with a grin that the controversy might lead him to be pictured in a role that few people ever put him in—the great saver of money and the one watchdog on the pockets of the people.

At one news conference he went into a discussion of inflation, relating how a friend complained about paying a high price for strawberries out of season. Months later he started talking about inflation again and told the same story, only this time the friend had bought asparagus.

He laughed with reporters when one of them

asked if this was the same man who got stuck for the strawberries.

Well, he said, it was a good story—and was true.

*   *   *

THE "RUMOR FACTORY"

Naive White House guests who sought to pry information from the President concerning confidential matters frequently received straight-faced answers that were the joking fantasy in which the President loved to indulge. Soon after the Doolittle raid on Tokyo, "a sweet young thing" (his phrase) who was a dinner guest at the White House wanted to know where the bombing planes came from. He told her they came from Shangri-La, and a famous phrase was born.

"A delightful little lady" who was a dinner guest at the White House the evening General MacArthur reached Australia from Corregidor, had her question rewarded with an explanation that MacArthur had taken a rowboat, disguised himself as a fisherman and slipped by Japanese warships in Manila Bay. And then, the President explained, General MacArthur rowed the 2,500 miles to Australia.

The President, confiding the story with glee to newspapermen, said the lady and some other dinner guests had really believed him.

To this, Stephen T. Early, the Presidential secretary, rejoined audibly, "That's the rumor factory for you," and the President had himself another laugh, for "rumor factory" was the appellation he himself had given Washington a few days before, in criticizing residents for spreading false reports about the war.

*   *   *

A FAMILY CONFLICT

In early days of the war, when government bureaus were mushrooming in Washington, reporters asked at a Presidential press conference if something couldn't be done about overlapping press conferences, pointing out that two or three bold officials had called conferences at 10:30 a.m. on Friday. That was the hour of the President's usual meeting with the press.

"Yes, Mrs. Roosevelt did once," a woman reporter observed. At this the President threw back his head and roared a laugh.

Sometime later, when the President, annoyed by some columnar references to him, termed columnists "excrescences," he grinned when he was

reminded that he had forgotten Mrs. Roosevelt's *My Day*.

*   *   *

THE GIRL REPORTER

Lee Carson, the famous woman reporter of International News Service, tells this story:

"Once upon a time when war was merely a big black cloud hanging heavily over the nation,. I authored a daily column called *F.D.R.'s Day* which went fairly hog-wild on revealing what goes on behind-the-scenes at the White House, including such details as how the President prefers old-fashioned cocktails before dinner, liked to work in his shirtsleeves, considered himself a shark at poker and exploded with a loud, healthy bang when someone or something got his dander up.

"Unfortunately war and censorship hung up the 'Out for the Duration Sign' on *F.D.R.'s Day* but it did bring about a highly informal introduction to the Great Man himself before its untimely demise.

"*F.D.R.'s Day* was a mere stripling when the collision of President and author occurred. Prior to this occasion my agents had whispered that the august **Chief** Executive now referred to me as his 'Blond Biographer' and, upon occasion, as 'a very snoopy party.'

"The latter description undoubtedly fitted like a glove upon the occasion of our first off-the-record, in-the-lodge meeting. I was reading the Presidential correspondence upside down, crooking my neck only a little, when opportunity knocked.

"As an inveterate reader of mail-on-desks upside-down I was deeply engossed in three letters, well written-upon, lying in front of Mr. Roosevelt during one of his weekly news conferences. There had been some cross-fire going on between President and press on taxes but I was concentrating on the letters when suddenly I realized the pressure caused by some 200 fellow correspondents edging ever closer to the Chief Executive's desk, was no longer. Neither was the cross-fire.

"Glancing quickly up I discovered that the big, oval office was being rapidly emptied of newsmen and, taking a quick peek at the President, realized that he was intensely interested in my progress with his mail. Leaping straight up in the air eight feet and back four I stared in horror at Mr. Roosevelt and his secretariat. There was a loud boom of laughter.

" 'Come here, Lee,' chuckled Presidential Secretary Steve Early. But my feet moved not and
my head did spin. Then the President waggled
a beckoning forefinger. This was hard to believe, even if I was seeing it with my own eyes.
No girl ever expects the President of the United
States to waggle a finger at her.

"Gingerly and with great effort I propelled
myself forward, stumbled over and past a row
of chairs and found myself leaning confiden-
tially into Mr. Roosevelt's face. Next I distinctly
heard him say something about putting him to
bed too late the previous evening.

" 'What?' said I, rapidly reviewing in my mind
the previous evening which included lots of
things but putting the President to bed was not
one of them. The President repeated, enunciat-
ing every word carefully.

" 'Oh, did I?' said I, vaguely, wondering what
he was talking about.

" 'As a matter of fact,' continued the President,
'last night's schedule did include staying up
until all hours getting some paper work cleaned
up, but everyone in the White House chose that
particular evening to be very busy, very absent,
very much with headache or just plain missing.
So there wasn't much to do,' he explained, wist-
fully, 'except autograph a few books and go to
bed.'

"Being nothing if not a great little one to take
advantage of a situation and this was A Situation, I thought immediately of the bang-up opportunity presenting itself to get a first-hand
item for *F.D.R.'s Day*.

" 'Sorry about last night, sir,' said I sweetly,
'what are you doing tonight?'

"The moment it was out, followed by a clap of
Presidential laughter, I recognized the question
from an old, old gag of the same name.

"Tonight, laughed the President, he was going
to make up for last night's idleness, but why not
ask again sometime?

"I managed a thin, dim grin through the rapidly reddening decor of my face and muttered
something about 'Yes, oh yes, to be sure, to be
sure,' stretched out a hand, felt it shaken firmly
and looked around for the nearest exit.

"After hiking uneasily over mile after mile of
deep-piled carpet I reached the door of the Executive Office, turned, got a final wave, grin and
nod, and loped out.

"At the next Presidential conference I took up
a well-concealed position behind a solid citizen

representing the *New York Times*. But the President had X-ray eyes. The boys still want to know
why he gave me that solemn, slow wink."

* * *

A "HEADACHE REMEDY"

Last public function attended by the President was the annual dinner of the White House
Correspondents' Association. He shook with
laughter at the entertainers' gags and wound up
the program with a gag of his own. Looking
around with a knowing expression at the drinking glasses on the correspondents' tables, he said
that "in the interest of humanity" he was can-
celling the press conference scheduled for the
following morning.

At this dinner, Danny Kaye led the crowd in a
song and begged everybody present to bark like
a dog. F.D.R.'s loud, spirited "Arf, Arf!" could
be clearly heard around the main table.

At an earlier correspondents' dinner, in January, F.D.R. laughed loudly when Jack Benny
apologized for his informal appearance by saying "I'm wearing a Hart, Schaffner & Marx suit,
and this shirt and tie—I got them at Montgom-
ery, Roosevelt and Ward."

Perhaps the biggest laugh ever given F.D.R.
and other guests at a correspondents' dinner by
any gag-line was one sprung by Bob Hope, in
1944. He said, "Dewey has his eye on the Presidential chair, but look what Roosevelt has on it."

Incidentally, F.D.R.'s chair in his Presidential
office at the White House, was the same one used
by President Hoover. F.D.R. worked at a different desk, but kept the same chair.

* * *

IDEAS BEFORE FORCE

F.D.R. used this story to illustrate a point:

"Two Chinese coolies who were arguing heatedly in the midst of a crowd. A stranger expressed
surprise that no blows were being struck. His
Chinese friend replied: 'The man who strikes
first admits that his ideas have given out.'"

* * *

ON HIS DESK

The cluttered Presidential desk at which
F.D.R. faced the reporters in the White House
press conferences, was often referred to in stories
and shown in pictures. Reporters were permitted
to make an inventory of the desk top and drawers
after F.D.R.'s death, and came up with this list:

On top, a dozen donkey emblems of the Democratic Party; four elephant symbols of the Re-

publican Party; six pigs, six dogs, three bears, one rabbit, one grinning figure of a Chinese holding a tremendous stomach. Two lighters, and three silver match boxes. A magnifying glass, a clock, a barometer, a thermometer, a lamp, a piece of wood of unusual shape, a desk lamp, a rack of blank cards upon which he was wont to scribble notes; carafe and two water glasses on a wooden tray.

Also, at one side were pictures in color, in a red leather frame, of the four Roosevelt sons in uniform. Matching it at the opposite side of the desk was a frame in which the daily list of engagements was kept. On a desk blotter was a black marble desk set inscribed Christmas, 1929, which F.D.R. brought from Albany. It had two fountain pens, several pencils and bottle of India ink the President used in signing letters and documents of historic importance. Nearby were other ink bottles, a small silver box, an early Chinese perfume bottle, a bronze Coast and Geodetic Survey marker, and a calendar.

In one drawer were more donkeys, letter openers, cancelled stamps for the Presidential collection, pins, ash trays, paper clips, rubber bands, a Lions Club badge, shamrocks, a package of headache pills.

Another drawer held a comb and brush, handkerchiefs, a mirror, cigarets, a shoe horn.

A red bowl out of which the President fed his pet Scottie, Fala, was on the floor beside the desk. Near it were a stuffed sock and a red rubber ball with which the Scottie liked to play.

Pictures of the sea and the inland waters were on the walls. Within one large frame, an early packet-boat steamed up Mr. Roosevelt's beloved Hudson.

*   *   *

F.D.R. AND THE PRESS

Like most of the reporters who covered it, F.D.R. thought being assigned to the White House outranked any other job in newspaperdom. When a reporter who had been given another and better-paid assignment, attended his last conference, the President winked at him and said: "Well, leaving the White House? Undoubtedly a demotion."

Although he rebuked various newspapers and newspaperman on particular occasions, he carried on the friendliest of relations with hundreds of reporters and publishers. Even publishers of opposition papers were invited with their wives to be guests at the White House. Whether the paper he worked for was editorially pro or anti,

an ill White House correspondent was likely to be the recipient of flowers from the Roosevelt greenhouse and other kind and thoughtful attentions were shown.

At one time or another most of the newspapers in the United States opposed F.D.R. on some issue. The fact that he continued to be re-elected was misread by some inept observers as evidence the newspapers had lost their influence. F.D.R. knew this wasn't so. He understood better than many of the men around him that while the newspapers might be criticising him in small space in their editorial pages, they were devoting full play in the front page to his own statements; and that was what was important. As W. T. Huddle pointed out in a letter to the *Saturday Review of Literature* before Roosevelt's death:

"Probably the President has been given, free, gratis, and for nothing, more front-page publicity than any two prior occupants of the White House, for several reasons: his New Deal social reform programs have been on the side of the sensational, against a conservative background, and were especially newsworthy for mass consumption; Mr. Roosevelt already has been thus publicized continuously for 12 years—fifty per cent longer than other durable Presidents; newspaper circulations are appreciably larger than in the past.

"Even trivia such as 'Fala's a Father,' commands front-page position, with one-column heads.

"So important is 'name publicity' to many larger advertisers that they employ writers to supply newspapers with editorial matter containing one or more name mentions only lightly perfumed with advertising propaganda. Mr. Roosevelt receives this type of publicity (a) in astronomical quantities, (b) continuously, (c) everywhere, (d) in the newspaper's prime position, the front page."

The President spoke his mind about the press in a letter in which he felicitated International News Service on its 25th anniversary:

"I personally find high satisfaction in the knowledge that it is possible in this land of ours for anyone to establish a newspaper or a news service and to enjoy the freedom of operation guaranteed by our fathers and which, I am glad to say, still prevails. I am glad, too, that our Government never has seen fit to subsidize a newspaper of a news service and I dare to make the prediction that it never will."

"PLENTY" BY PROCLAMATION

In his last press conference at the White House, F.D.R. spoke "off the record" about those, in and out of Congress, who think there is a remedy, through investigation or otherwise, for everything. The food situation was being discussed and a reporter asked:

"Do you think that a Congressional investigation would be advantageous and helpful?"

Roosevelt: "That's a tricky question."

Reporter: "It wasn't meant to be, sir."

Roosevelt: "But it is tricky. I just don't like to criticize Congress. I feel a little bit this way about it, and put this off the record—what can we find that we don't know already? I don't know. There's a good many people in the government that can tell you the thing in a half hour. I think the legislative body thinks I should pass a resolution that the amount of food in the country would be just twice what it is. Maybe they would find something useful about it. I would be delighted if they did."

*   *   *

PUTTING IT OVER

Once when a member who had a lesser post in the administration was making some big promises to the press about the solution of a pressing problem, F.D.R. was reminded of a story of a little boy who went through offices in a New York skyscraper proffering picture postcards at 10 cents each.

"What are you going to do with the money?" he was asked.

"I'm raising $1,000,000 for the Red Cross," he answered gravely.

"A million dollars! All by yourself?" the inquirer responded.

"No, sir," the tot replied, "There's another little boy helping me."

*   *   *

HIS DAILY LIFE

Robert Considine, famous International News Service correspondent and co-author of *30 Seconds Over Tokyo*, wrote an intimate closeup of F.D.R. for INS, in 1938, from which the following is taken:

"The White House swimming pool, and a little rubbing room, are the elixirs of the Chief Executive. At 5:30 o'clock each afternoon he leaves his office for what is called the West Terrace. The room is nearly filled by the pool. The tank is 50 feet long, 15 feet wide, five feet deep at the shallow end and nine at the other.

"The President is an excellent swimmer. His brawny shoulders, full of supple muscles, can pull him through the water at a good clip. He uses the breast-stroke mostly, but is equally proficient with the "crawl" and the backstroke. He likes to do it, but in respect to Dr. Ross McIntyre's wishes, he has dispensed with under-water swimming, to guard against sinus trouble.

"The President invented his own system of exercising in the water during his long stern fight for health at Warm Spring, Ga. The specific gravity of the Warm Springs water is almost as high as sea water.

"Swimming and massaging must fill the President's desire now for an active sports life. When he was here as Assistant Secretary of the Navy, in war times, he played a lot of golf at Chevy Chase. He was a little uncertain around the greens, but still was a middle 80 linksman.

"When he is on vacation, deep-sea fishing takes the place of swimming. He exhausts the men who go out with him, staying in a small boat sometimes from 9 in the morning until after dark. He is all man when he hooks a big one, his tremendous grip and great back muscles serving him well. On trips where no fishing is available he confines his "workouts" to massages. Chubby, strong-handed George Fox, a Navy C. P. O., can give him the muscular equivalent of a long swim, or a round of golf, or a couple of sets of tennis.

"Sometimes he brings along to the swimming pool whoever happens to be the last person he has to see at the office. There's a guest's dressing room just off the President's own rub-down and dressing room, with spare suits and caps.

"After a half hour in the pool he goes into his small rubbing room with baldish Dr. McIntyre, his personal physician, and Fox then gives him a brisk rub-down on the training table. Sometimes the President smokes a crumpled cigaret while this is going on. Occasionally he takes an infra-red lamp treatment, and at the end of the hour he is relaxed from his day's work and ready either for an exhausting evening of state functions or working in his model ship-filled study."

In 1945, Considine wrote this picture of the President's changed daily life:

"The President is leaner these days, as well as grayer of face and thinning hair. He's humanly proud of the new flatness of his stomach. His personal physician, Vice Admiral Ross T. McIntyre, has taken about 15 pounds off him—with the help of the President's many worries.

"McIntyre watches him like a hawk, to keep his weight (182) from falling off any more. Recently he has ordered the President to take a tall glass of milk, with an egg whippéd up in it, about 4:30 each afternoon.

"As has been his custom for years, the President smokes 'too much.' Like everybody else in the country, he has had a little trouble getting his favorite brand of cigarettes.

"He seldom gets a crack at the swimming pool which his one-time intimate, and now arch-foe, Joseph Patterson, built for him in the wing that leads from the Executive Office to the White House.

"Admiral McIntyre's assistant, Lieut. Comdr. George Fox, still gives the President an almost daily rubdown, however, usually about 6:30 P. M., when he quits his office and heads for the White House.

"The President takes what is called a 'deep' rub, smokes a cigarette or two on the rubbing table, in a little room off the pool, while the strong-handed officer kneads him, and then goes on to the White House.

"He usually takes a Martini before dinner, and his dinners are quiet and full of relaxing small talk by his closest friends—often the Harry Hopkinses—and his family. His daughter, Anna Boettiger, is living in the White House now and he finds her very stimulating at this time of day.

"He works every night. There may be a movie over in the plushy projection room in the East Wing of the White House.

"He does most of his paper work in the evenings in his quiet, oval, ship-lined study on the second floor of the mansion.

"Late at night his valet, 70-year-old John Mays, a colored man who has worked at the White House for thirty years, and who doubles as doorman when the President doesn't need him, helps him with the job of retiring.

"The President then sits propped up in bed, has a chance to look over the afternoon papers and may skip through a magazine—though never a book any more. He may even make a phone call or two.

"About midnight, while the military guards pace outside the big iron fence of the White House, he snaps out his bedlight and goes to sleep. Come war, pestilence and worry enough to break the health of a weight-lifter, Roosevelt can always sleep. He sleeps like a baby for eight hours a night.

"Mays comes in at 8:30 A. M. to awaken him. He brings along four morning papers—Washington, New York, Baltimore and Philadelphia—and then lugs in breakfast on a tray. Unless Admiral McIntyre had something to say about it, the President would have orange juice and scrambled eggs every morning. He breakfasts alone, in bed.

"Steve Early, Harry Hopkins and occasionally Admiral Leahy come to his bedroom after breakfast, to give him an idea of his appointments for the morning and to bring him up to date on the latest foreign and domestic developments.

"The President then bathes, shaves and dresses and goes over to the office about 10 o'clock. His official day begins with perhaps a visit from, or a phone call to, a Cabinet officer or military chieftain.

"Then it's a round of callers, ranging from governors of states to ambassadors, from military men to Congressional leaders. Between their comings and goings he makes great use of the lone telephone on his desk.

"A few months ago he gave up the practice of having someone share his rolling steam-table lunch that is wheeled in at 12:30, but to see everybody he wants to see these days he has had to go back to the habit. Lord Halifax had lunch with him the other day, eating gingerly off the pulled out armrest of the President's desk.

"Through the afternoon he sees sometimes a dozen more dignitaries, and is always a little behind on his schedule, for if he likes a man, or is interested in what he is saying, he'll keep him beyond the allotted time.

"Recently he has taken a few auto rides around Washington in the late afternoon—has been out to the Naval Hospital to see ex-Secretary Cordell Hull a few times.

"He sees the press on Tuesdays and Fridays and is his old self when the men storm in and fill the chairless room. He doesn't hear quite as well as he once did.

"He can still hedge as neatly as ever on the tough questions. There are always some laughs during the news conference, which gives him a kick."

*   *   *

HAD NAVY IN BLOOD

As a youngster, F.D.R. used to say, "I don't want to go to school, I want to go to sea." Then he made Annapolis his objective. But like George Washington, who would have been a British naval officer if his mother hadn't objected to the long absences a naval career will entail, F.D.R. was talked out of it by his folks. In 1913, when he was given the job of Assistant Secretary of the Navy, he told friends, "I'd rather have it then any other in public life."

If Washington had become a British naval officer, there might not have been a winning commander-in-chief in the Revolution. And it was fortunate for the Navy that it had there a Navy-minded President who began in 1938 to build up a big fleet for the war ahead. Also, it was fortunate F.D.R. ignored protests made by Britain in 1938 against the disturbance of naval equality between the two nations resulting from the Roosevelt naval construction program.

The President regularly received catalogues from two dozen or more booksellers specializing in works relating to ships and the seas, pored over them and made purchases. He maintained a complete file of *United States Naval Institute Proceedings,* and always had around him such works as Lovette's *Naval Customs, Traditions and Usage* and naval histories.

* * *

LIKED HULL STORY

The President recalled with relish that in the first few hours after the Pearl Harbor sneak attack, when he and his foreign-policy advisers meditated whether to declare war on Germany and its European satellites or await their anticipated action, Secretary Hull told a story:

"Down in our country in Tennessee we had a Negro boy who liked to think he was the best mule trainer in the country. He boasted he had never been thrown and could break the roughest mule that could be brought to him. Other boys finally got tired of his boasting and they fetched in a scientific, double-back action mule. Two minutes after the self-constituted champion mounted the mule he was picking himself up from the ground. He wasn't feazed, however. He said: 'That's the way to break a mule. When you figger he going to throw you, you just get off.'"

* * *

A "CHOICE" STORY

A story said to be one of Roosevelt's favorites was one told by Hull about the young Tennessee mountain lad who courted a girl for what, by mountain standards, was an unconsciously long time. One evening the girl's father stopped the boy and said: "You been courtin' my gal for a long time now. Are your intentions honorable?" The lad blushed, then looked up brightly. "You mean I got a choice?"

RESPONSE TO ASTOR

After President Roosevelt spent some summer days fishing from Vincent Astor's yacht, *Nourmahal,* he was once invited to take a winter cruise.

"Oh, don't put that big thing in commission in winter just for me," F.D.R. responded.

"Mr. President, the *Nourmahal* is in commission all year around," Astor replied.

"Well," rejoined the President with a grin, "I guess we'll have to raise taxes on the rich again."

* * *

HOW HE WON A CASE

This is one of the stories F.D.R. told about his early days in law practice. In a civil suit, the opposing counsel was a veteran who was an unusually effective jury pleader. F.D.R. realized as he listened to the veteran's summing up that he could not match it for persuasiveness. The veteran, however, made a mistake: he continued his oration for more than an hour, and F.D.R. saw the jury became restless and lose interest. So, playing a hunch when his turn came, Roosevelt arose and said, "Gentlemen, you have heard the evidence. You also have listened to my distinguished colleague, a brilliant lawyer. If you believe him, and disbelieve the evidence, you will have to decide in his favor. That is all I have to say."

The jury was out five minutes and brought in a verdict for Roosevelt's client.

* * *

CUT DIPLOMATIC RED TAPE

In accordance with generations-old diplomatic procedure, the representative of a foreign country, before being actually presented to the President, exchanged formal speeches with him. F.D.R. broke with tradition in this respect also. For on one occasion, instead of repeating the stilted formal phrases, the President greeted the newly accredited diplomat by sticking out his hand and saying, "Mr. Minister, I've heard your remarks and you've heard mine, so let's dispense with the speeches and have a chat."

* * *

LOVED SCRAMBLED EGGS

The President's favorite dish was scrambled eggs. He never seemed to tire of it. On Sunday nights, when groups of intimates were invited to the White House for supper, Mrs. Roosevelt made these at the dinner table in a chafing dish. F.D.R. also was fond of whitefish. He ate with a big appetite up until his last months, when his lack of appetite was one undeniable symptom of his failing health. He had few food dislikes. Once, however, in a strong note to Damon Runyon, another heckler of *Popeye's* favorite dish, he expressed his apathy to spinach.

But when he invited several hundred Washington correspondents and their wives to be White House guests, the "eats" were bologna sandwiches with plenty of beer. He ate with as much gusto as any of them. Fare at the White House table was generally simple. One distinguished man who spent several days as a house guest at the White House came away complaining of hunger.

* * *

MET ELEANOR WHEN 15

Walter Winchell wrote the following things in a revealing closeup of F.D.R., based on close acquaintance with the President:

"He met his wife at a dance when he was 15 years old and she was 12. They announced their engagement seven years later. The White House wasn't anything new to Franklin and Eleanor Roosevelt when he became President; they often spent weeks there as guests of Teddy Roosevelt.

"F.D.R. has always been a wizard politician. When he ran for state senator he toured his county in a car. At that time farmers were prejudiced against the new fangled automobiles, so he made certain that his car had an occasional breakdown which necessitated its rescue by horses.

"German police once arrested F.D.R. During his 'teens he made a bicycle tour of Germany, and violated some minor traffic regulations. As a youth, Roosevelt made many trips to Europe with his mother. He first crossed the Atlantic when he was two.

"While serving as Assistant Secretary of the Navy during the last war, a new type of mine was brought to his attention by a little known scientist. F.D.R. urged the Allies to adopt the new mine, and finally convinced them. The new weapon promptly clicked. The mine succeeded in keeping Germany's fleet bottled up in the North Sea. It was one of the vital factors in winning the war.

"He is an expert poker player. When he gets a chance to play he enjoys originating variations of the game.

"F.D.R. is an expert swimmer and enjoys ducking friends and engaging in wrestling matches with those who share the pool with him."

AT RIGHT, F.D.R. IN BOYHOOD, A YEAR OR TWO BEFORE HE MET ELEANOR FIRST AT A DANCE.

IN HIS OWN WORDS

The War and the Post-War World

THE GOAL

It would be inconceivable—it would, indeed, be sacrilegious—if this nation and the world did not attain some real, lasting good out of all these efforts and sufferings and bloodshed and death. The men in our armed forces want a lasting peace and, equally, they want permanent employment for themselves, their families and their neighbors when they are mustered out at the end of the war.

We fight to retain a great past—and we fight to gain a greater future. Today the United Nations are the mightiest coalition in history. They can and must remain united for the maintenance of the peace by preventing any attempt to rearm in Germany, in Japan, in Italy, or in any other nation that seeks to violate the Tenth Commandment—"Thou shalt not covet."—*Message to Congress, Jan. 7, 1943.*

*   *   *

SHALL IT BE AGAIN?

There are a few people in this country who, when the collapse of the Axis begins, will tell our people that we are safe once more; that we can tell the rest of the world to "stew in its own juice"; that never again will we help to pull the "other fellow's chestnuts from the fire"; that the future of civilization can jolly well take care of itself in so far as we are concerned. But it is useless to win battles if the cause for which we fight these battles is lost. It is useless to win a war unless it stays won. We, therefore, fight for the restoration and perpetuation of faith and hope and peace throughout the world.—*Talk to the nation, Oct. 12, 1942.*

*   *   *

"LET US MOVE FORWARD"

The once powerful, malignant Nazi state is crumbling, the Japanese war lords are receiving, in their own homeland, the retribution for which they asked when they attacked Pearl Harbor.

But the mere conquest of our enemies is not enough.

We must go on to do all in our power to conquer the doubts and the fears, the ignorance and the greed, which made this horror possible.

Thomas Jefferson, himself a distinguished scientist, once spoke of the "brotherly spirit of science which unites into one family all its votaries of whatever grade and however widely dispersed throughout the different quarters of the globe."

Today, science has brought all the different quarters of the globe so close together that it is impossible to isolate them one from another.

Today we are faced with the preeminent fact that, if civilization is to survive, we must cultivate the science of human relationships—the ability of all peoples, of all kinds, to live together and work together, in the same world, at peace.

Let me assure you that my hand is the steadier for the work that is to be done, that I move more firmly into the task, knowing that you—millions and millions of you—are joined with me in the resolve to make this work endure.—*From the manuscript of his last address, which he completed the night before his death, for delivery as a tribute to Thomas Jefferson. The last words of the address were:*

The only limit to our realization of tomorrow will be our doubts of today. Let us move forward with strong and active faith.

*   *   *

RIGHTS OF SMALL NATIONS

I like to think that the history of the Philippine Islands in the last 44 years provides in a very real sense a pattern for the future of other small nations and peoples of the world. It is a pattern of what men of good will look forward to in the future—a pattern of global civilization which recognizes no limitations of religion or of creed or of race.—*Address, Nov. 15, 1942.*

*   *   *

INTERNATIONAL ORGANIZATION

It is clear that, if the world organization is to have any reality at all, our representative must be endowed in advance by the people themselves, by constitutional means through their representatives in the Congress, with authority to act.

If we do not catch the international felon when we have our hands on him, if we let him get away with his loot because the town council has not passed an ordinance authorizing his arrest, then we are not doing our share to prevent another world war. The people of the nation want their government to act, and not merely to talk, whenever and wherever there is a threat to world peace.—*Foreign Policy Association speech, Oct. 23, 1944.*

* * *

WHY WE FIGHT

To win this war wholeheartedly, unequivocally and as quickly as we can is our task of the first importance. To win this war in such a way that there be no further world wars in the foreseeable future is our second objective. To provide occupations, and to provide a decent standard of living for our men in the armed forces after the war, and for all Americans, are the final objectives.—*Speech accepting the Presidential nomination, July 11, 1944.*

* * *

ECONOMIC CO-OPERATION

It is time for the United States to take the lead in establishing the principle of economic co-operation as the foundation for expanded world trade.

We have done a good deal in those directions in the last 10 years under the Trade Agreements Act of 1934 and through the stabilization fund operated by our Treasury.

A good start has been made. The United Nations' monetary conference at Bretton Woods has taken a long step forward on a matter of great importance to all.—*Report to Congress on Bretton Woods, Feb. 12, 1945.*

* * *

WE MUST START SOMEWHERE

For the second time in the lives of most of us, this generation is face to face with the objective of preventing wars. To meet that objective, the nations of the world will either have a plan or they will not. The groundwork of a plan has now been furnished, and has been submitted to humanity for discussion and decision.

No plan is perfect. Whatever is adopted at San Francisco will doubtless have to be amended time and again over the years, just as our own Constitution has been.

I am confident that the Congress and the American people will accept the results of this conference as the beginning of a permanent structure of peace upon which we can begin to build, under God, that better world in which our children and grandchildren, yours and mine, the children and grandchildren of the whole world must live and can live. — *Report on the Yalta Conference, March 1, 1945* [*his last address to Congress.*]

* * *

"THERE IS NO SECURITY"

There is no such thing as security for any nation—or any individual—in a world ruled by the principles of gangsterism. There is no such thing as impregnable defense against powerful aggressors who sneak up in the dark and strike without warning. We have learned that our ocean-girt hemisphere is not immune from severe attack—that we cannot measure our safety in terms of miles on any map.

We may acknowledge that our enemies have performed a brilliant feat of deception, perfectly timed and executed with great skill. It was a thoroughly dishonorable deed, but we must face the fact that modern warfare as conducted in the Nazi manner is a dirty business. We don't like it—we didn't want to get in it—but we are in it and we're going to fight it with everything we've got.

We are going to win the war, and we are going to win the peace that follows. And in the dark hours of this day—and through dark days that may be yet to come—we will know that the vast majority of the members of the human race are on our side. Many of them are fighting with us. All of them are praying for us. For, in representing our cause, we represent theirs as well—our hope and their hope for liberty under God.—*Radio talk to the nation, Dec. 9, 1941.*

* * *

"NOT AS OSTRICHES"

We have learned that we cannot live alone, at peace; that our own well-being is dependent upon the well-being of other nations, far away.

We have learned that we must live as men, and not as ostriches, nor as dogs in the manger.

We have learned to be citizens of the world, members of the human community.

We have learned the simple truth, as Emerson said, that "the only way to have a friend is to be one."

We can gain no lasting peace if we approach it with suspicion and mistrust—or with fear.

We can gain it only if we proceed with the

understanding and the confidence and the courage which flow from conviction.—*Fourth inaugural address, Jan. 20, 1945.*

*   *   *

THE FOUR FREEDOMS

In the future days, which we seek to make secure, we look forward to a world founded upon four essential human freedoms.

The first is freedom of speech and expression—everywhere in the world.

The second is freedom of every person to worship God in his own way—everywhere in the world.

The third is freedom from want—which, translated into world terms, means economic understandings which will secure to every nation a healthy peacetime life for its inhabitants—everywhere in the world.

The fourth is freedom from fear—which, translated into world terms, means a world-wide reduction of armaments to such a point and in such a thorough fashion that no nation will be in a position to commit an act of physical aggression against any neighbor—anywhere in the world.—*Message to Congress, Jan. 6, 1941.*

*   *   *

WHAT VICTORY WILL MEAN

I think that the victory of the American people and their allies in this war will be far more than a victory against fascism and reaction and the dead hand of despotism of the past. The victory of the American people and their allies in this war will be a victory for democracy. It will constitute such an affirmation of the strength and power and vitality of government by the people as history has never before witnessed.—*Speech in Washington, Sept. 23, 1944.*

Foreign Policy 1933-41

THE GOOD NEIGHBOR

In the field of world policy, I would dedicate this nation to the policy of the good neighbor—the neighbor who resolutely respects himself and, because he does so, respects the rights of others—the neighbor who respects his obligations and respects the sanctity of his agreements in and with a world of neighbors.—*First inaugural address, March 4, 1933.*

*   *   *

RECOGNITION OF SOVIET RUSSIA

I believe sincerely that the most impelling motive that has lain behind the conversations which were successfully concluded yesterday between Russia and the United States was the desire of both countries for peace and for the strengthening of the peaceful purposes of the civilized world.

It will interest you to know that in the year 1809 the President of the United States, Thomas Jefferson, wrote as follows to his Russian friend, M. Dashkoff:

"Russia and the United States being in character and practice essentially pacific, a common interest in the rights of peaceable nations gives us a common cause in their maintenance."

In this spirit of Thomas Jefferson, Mr. Litvinov and I believe that through the resumption of normal relations the prospects of peace over all the world are greatly strengthened.—*Speech at Savannah, Georgia, Nov. 19, 1933.*

*   *   *

"A RENDEZVOUS WITH DESTINY"

There is a mysterious cycle in human events. To some generations much is given. Of other generations much is expected. This generation of Americans has a rendezvous with destiny.

In this world of ours in other lands, there are some people, who, in times past, have lived and fought for freedom, and seem to have grown too weary to carry on the fight. They have sold their heritage of freedom for the illusion of a living. They have yielded their democracy.

I believe in my heart that only our success can stir their ancient hope. They begin to know that here in America we are waging a great and successful war. It is not alone a war against want and destitution and economic demoralization. It is more than that; it is a war for the survival of democracy. We are fighting to save a great and precious form of government for ourselves and for the world.—*Convention address at Philadelphia, June 27, 1936.*

*   *   *

QUARANTINE THE AGGRESSORS!

The peace, the freedom and the security of 90 per cent of the population of the world is being jeopardized by the remaining 10 per cent who are threatening a breakdown of all international order and law. When an epidemic of physical disease starts to spread, the community approves and joins in a quarantine of the patients in order to protect the health of the community against the spread of the disease.

War is a contagion, whether it be declared or undeclared. It can engulf states and peoples remote from the original scene of hostilities. We cannot have complete protection in a world of disorder in which confidence and security have broken down.—*From his historic "Quarantine" speech at Chicago, Oct. 5, 1937.*

* * *

"NO PEACE WITH FASCISM"

It is becoming increasingly clear that peace by fear has no higher or more enduring quality than peace by the sword.

There can be no peace if the reign of law is to be replaced by a recurrent sanctification of sheer force. There can be no peace if national policy adopts as a deliberate instrument the dispersion all over the world of millions of helpless and persecuted wanderers with no place to lay their heads.

There can be no peace if humble men and women are not free to think their own thoughts, to express their own feelings, to worship God.

There can be no peace if economic resources that ought to be devoted to social and economic reconstruction are to be diverted to an intensified competition in armaments which will merely heighten the suspicions and fears and threaten the economic prosperity of each and every nation.—*Address to Herald-Tribune Forum, Oct. 27, 1938.*

* * *

"NO NATION CAN BE SAFE"

The world has grown so small and weapons of attack so swift that no nation can be safe in its will to peace so long as any other powerful nation refuses to settle its grievances at the council table.—*Message to Congress, Jan. 1, 1939.*

* * *

"ALL THE SAME FIGHT"

There comes a time in the affairs of men when they must prepare to defend, not their homes alone, but the tenets of faith and humanity on which their churches, their governments and their very civilization are founded. The defense of religion, of democracy and good faith among nations is all the same fight. To save one we must now make up our minds to save all.—*Message to Congress, Jan. 1, 1939.*

ONE WORLD

It is easy for you and for me to shrug our shoulders and to say that conflicts taking place thousands of miles from the continental United States, and, indeed, thousands of miles from the whole American Hemisphere, do not seriously affect the Americas—and that all the United States has to do is to ignore them and go about its own business.

Passionately though we may desire detachment, we are forced to realize that every word that comes through the air, every ship that sails the sea, every battle that is fought does affect the American future.—*Radio talk to the nation, Sept. 3, 1939.*

* * *

"DAGGER IN THE BACK"

"The government of Italy has now chosen to preserve what it terms its 'freedom of action' and to fulfill what it states are its promises to Germany. In so doing, it has manifested disregard for the rights and security of other nations, disregard for the lives of the peoples of those nations which are directly threatened by this spread of the war; and has evidenced its unwillingness to find the means through pacific negotiations for the satisfaction of what it believes are its legitimate aspirations. On this tenth day of June, 1940, the hand that held the dagger has struck it into the back of its neighbor."—*Address at Charlottesville, Va., June 10, 1940.*

* * *

THE CHOICE WE FACE

We face one of the great choices of history.

It is not alone a choice of government by the people versus dictatorship.

It is not alone a choice of freedom versus slavery.

It is not alone a choice between moving forward and falling back.

It is all of these rolled into one.

It is the continuance of civilization as we know it versus the ultimate destruction of all that we have held dear—religion against godlessness; the ideal of justice against the practice of force; moral decency versus the firing squad; courage to speak out, and to act, versus the false lullaby of appeasement.—*Address to Democratic National Convention, July 19, 1940.*

* * *

THE ARSENAL OF DEMOCRACY

The light of democracy must be kept burning. To the perpetuation of this light, each must do his own share. The single effort of one individual may seem very small. But there are 130,000,000 individuals over here. There are many more millions in Britain and elsewhere bravely shielding the great flame of democracy from the blackout of barbarism. It is not enough for us merely to trim the wick, or polish the glass. The time has come when we must provide the fuel in ever-increasing amounts to keep the flame alight.

The British people and their Grecian allies need ships. From America, they will get ships. They need planes. From America, they will get planes. They need food. From America, they will get food. They need tanks and guns and ammunition and supplies of all kinds. From America, they will get tanks and guns and ammunition and supplies of all kinds.

China likewise expresses the magnificent will of millions of plain people to resist the dismemberment of their nation. China, through the generalissimo, Chiang Kai-Shek, asks our help. America has said that China shall have our help.

Our country is going to be what our people have proclaimed it must be — the arsenal of democracy. — *Address at White House correspondents' dinner, March 15, 1941.*

*   *   *

"THE ONLY THING WE HAVE TO FEAR"

There are some timid ones among us who say that we must preserve peace at any price—lest we lose our liberties forever. To them I say: never in the history of the world has a nation lost its democracy by a successful struggle to defend its democracy. We must not be defeated by the fear of the very danger which we are preparing to resist. Our freedom has shown its ability to survive war, but it would never survive surrender. "The only thing we have to fear is fear itself."—*Address, proclaiming an unlimited national emergency, May 27, 1941.*

[The last phrase was a quotation from his first inaugural address, in which he said:

"This great nation will endure as it has endured, will revive and will prosper. So first of all, let me assert my firm belief that the only thing we have to fear is fear itself— nameless, unreasoning, unjustified terror which paralyzes needed efforts to convert retreat into advance."]

*   *   *

NO HITLER-DOMINATED WORLD

Today the whole world is divided between human slavery and human freedom, between pagan brutality and the Christian ideal. We choose human freedom—which is the Christian ideal. No one of us can waver for a moment in his courage or his faith.

We will not accept a Hitler-dominated world. And we will not accept a world, like the post-war world of the 1920's, in which the seeds of Hitlerism can again be planted and allowed to grow.

We will accept only a world consecrated to freedom of speech and expression—freedom of every person to worship God in his own way— freedom from want—and freedom from terrorism.—*World-wide radio adress, May 27, 1941.*

Aria in Sydney, Australia, Sunday Sun.

THE NEW DEAL

"A FUNDAMENTAL CHANGE"

I believe that we are at the threshold of a fundamental change in our popular economic thought, that in the future we are going to think less about the producer and more about the consumer. Do what we may have to do to inject life into our ailing economic order, we cannot make it endure for long unless we can bring about a wiser, more equitable distribution of the national income.—*Address at Oglethorpe University, May 22, 1931.*

*   *   *

"A NEW DEAL"

I pledge you, I pledge myself, to a new deal for the American people. Let us all here assembled constitute ourselves prophets of a new order of competence and of courage. This is more than a political campaign: it is a call to arms. Give me your help, not to win votes alone, but to win in this crusade to restore America to its own people. —*Address accepting nomination to the Presidency, July 2, 1932.*

*   *   *

"PARTNERSHIP WITH GOVERNMENT"

It is wholly wrong to call the measure that we have taken government control of farming, industry, and transportation. It is rather a partnership between government and farming and industry and transportation, not partnership in profits, for the profits still go to the citizens, but rather a partnership in planning, and a partnership to see that the plans are carried out . . .

We are working toward a definite goal, which is to prevent the return of conditions which came very close to destroying what we call modern civilization. The actual accomplishment of our purpose cannot be attained in a day. Our policies are wholly within purposes for which our American constitutional government was established 150 years ago.—*Second "fireside chat," May 7, 1933.*

*   *   *

RELIEF, RECOVERY AND REFORM

In the consistent development of our previous efforts toward the saving and safeguarding of our national life, I have continued to recognize three related steps. The first was relief, because the primary concern of any Government dominated by the humane ideals of democracy is the simple principle that in a land of resources no one should be permitted to starve. Relief was and continues to be our first consideration. It calls for large expenditures and will continue in modified form to do so for a long time to come. We may as well recognize that fact. It comes from the paralysis that arose as the after-effect of that unfortunate decade characterized by a mad chase for unearned riches, and an unwillingness of leaders in almost every walk of life to look beyond their own schemes and speculations.

In our administration of relief we follow two principles: first, that direct giving shall, wherever possible, be supplemented by provision for useful and remunerative work and, second, that where families in their existing surroundings will in all human probability never find an opportunity for full self-maintenance, happiness and enjoyment, we shall try to give them a new chance in new surroundings.

The second step was recovery, and it is sufficient for me to ask each and every one of you to compare the situation in agriculture and in industry today and with what it was fifteen months ago.

At the same time we have recognized the necessity of reform and reconstruction—reform because much of our trouble today and in the past few years has been due to a lack of understanding of the elementary principles of justice and fairness by those in whom leadership in business and finance was placed—reconstruction because new conditions in our economic life as well as old but neglected conditions had to be corrected.—*Fireside chat, June 28, 1934.*

*   *   *

THE BASIS OF TRUE WEALTH

I need not tell you that true wealth is not a static thing. It is a living thing made out of the disposition of men to create and to distribute the good things of life with rising standards of living. Wealth grows when men co-operate; but it stagnates in an atmosphere of misunderstanding and misrepresentation.

Here, in America, the material means are at

hand for the growth of true wealth. It is in the spirit of American institutions that wealth should come as the reward of hard labor—hard labor, I repeat—of mind and hand. That is a pretty good definition of what we call the profit system. Its real fulfillment comes in the general recognition of the rights of each factor of the community.

It is not in the spirit of partisans, but it is in the spirit of partners, that America has progressed.—*In Washington, Oct. 24, 1934.*

* * *

TEST OF PROGRESS

"The test of our progress is not whether we add more to the abundance of those who have much; it is whether we provide enough for those who have too little."—*Message to Congress, Jan. 4, 1935.*

* * *

ON SOCIAL SECURITY

We can never insure one hundred per cent of the population against one hundred per cent of the hazards and vicissitudes of life, but we have tried to frame a law which will give some measure of protection to the average citizen and to his family against the loss of a job and against poverty-ridden old age.

This law, too, represents a cornerstone in a structure which is being built but is by no means complete. It is a structure intended to lessen the force of possible future depressions. It will act as a protection to future administrations against the necessity of going deeply into debt to furnish relief to the needy. The law will flatten out the peaks and valleys of deflation and of inflation. It is, in short, a law that will take care of human needs and at the same time provide for the United States an economic structure of vastly greater soundness.—*Statement upon signing the Social Security Act, Aug. 14, 1935.*

* * *

"RESULT OF MONOPOLY"

The net result of monopoly, the net result of economic and financial control in the hands of the few, has meant ownership of labor as a commodity.

If labor is to be a commodity in the United States, in the final analysis it means we shall become a nation of boarding houses instead of a nation of homes.

If our people ever submit to that, they will have said good-bye to their historic freedom. Men do not fight for boarding houses. They will fight for their homes.—*Address at Dallas, June 12, 1936.*

* * *

"ONE-THIRD OF THE NATION..."

Here is the challenge to our democracy: In this nation I see tens of millions of its citizens—a substantial part of its whole population—who at this very moment are denied the greater part of what the very lowest standards of today call the necessities of life.

I see millions of families trying to live on incomes so meager that the pall of family disaster hangs over them day by day.

I see millions whose daily lives in city and on farm continue under conditions labelled indecent by a so-called polite society half a century ago.

I see millions denied education, recreation, and the opportunity to better their lot and the lot of their children. I see millions lacking the means to buy the products of farm and factory and by their poverty denying work and productiveness to many other millions.

I see one-third of a nation ill-housed, ill-clad, ill-nourished.—*Second Inaugural Address, Jan. 20, 1937.*

* * *

THE FUNCTION OF GOVERNMENT

In our generation, a new idea has come to dominate thought about government, the idea that the resources of the nation can be made to produce a far higher standard of living for the masses of the people if only government is intelligent and energetic in giving the right direction to economic life.—*Constitution Day Address, Sept. 17, 1937.*

* * *

LABOR AND THE NEW DEAL

Organized labor as a whole has become stronger in membership, stronger in influence, and stronger in its capacity to serve the interests of the laboring man and woman and of society in general. . . . Much of this progress has been due, I like to think, to the one thing that this administration from the very beginning has insisted upon: the assurance to labor of the untrammeled right, not privilege, but right to organize and bargain collectively with its employers. That principle has now become firmly imbedded in the law of the land; it must remain as the foundation of industrial relations for all time.—*Speech to teamsters' convention, Sept. 11, 1940.*

"SIXTY MILLION JOBS"

I believe in free enterprise—and always have. I believe in the profit system—and always have. I believe that private enterprise can give full employment to our people. If anyone feels that my faith in our ability to provide sixty million peacetime jobs is fantastic, let him remember that some people thought the same thing about my demand in 1940 for fifty thousand airplanes. I believe in exceptional rewards for innovation, skill, and risk-taking by business.—*In Chicago, Oct. 28, 1944.*

Democracy

IT IS NOT STATIC

Democracy is not a static thing. It is an everlasting march. When our children grow up, they will still have problems to overcome. It is for us, however, manfully to set ourselves to the task of preparation for them, so that to some degree the difficulties they must overcome may weigh upon them less heavily.—*Address at Los Angeles, Oct. 1, 1935.*

*   *   *

HIS ANCHOR

My anchor is democracy—and more democracy. And, my friends, I am of the firm belief that the nation, by an overwhelming majority supports my opposition to the vesting of supreme power in the hands of any class, numerous but select.

I seek no change in the form of American government. Majority rule must be preserved as the safeguard of both liberty and civilization.

Under it property can be secured; under it abuses can end; under it order can be maintained —and all this for the simple, cogent reason that to the average of our citizenship can be brought a life of greater opportunity, of greater security, of greater happiness.—*Address at Roanoke Island, Aug. 18, 1937.*

*   *   *

A TEXT FOR ALL AMERICANS

I thought of preaching on a text, but I shall not. I shall only give you the text and I shall not preach on it. . . .

The text is this: Remember, remember always, that all of us, and you and I especially, are descended from immigrants and revolutionists. —*Remarks before the Daughters of the American Revolution, April 21, 1938.*

*   *   *

DEMOCRACY'S SAFEGUARD

Democracy cannot succeed unless those who express their choice are prepared to choose wisely. The real safeguard of democracy, therefore, is education. It has been well said that no system of government gives so much as a democracy.

Upon our educational system must largely depend the perpetuity of those institutions upon which freedom and our security rest. To prepare each citizen to choose wisely and to enable him to choose freely are paramount functions of the schools in a democracy.—*Education Week message, Sept. 27, 1938.*

*   *   *

A SINGLE UNITY

We are a nation of many nationalities, many races, many religions—bound together by a single unity, the unity of freedom and equality.

Whoever seeks to set one nationality against another, seeks to degrade all nationalities.

Whoever seeks to set one race against another, seeks to enslave all races. Whoever seeks to set one religion against another, seeks to destroy all religion.

I am fighting for a free America—for a country in which *all* men and women have equal rights to liberty and justice.

I am fighting, as I always have fought, for the rights of the little man as well as the big man— for the weak as well as the strong, for those who are helpless as well as for those who can help themselves.—*In New York, Nov. 1, 1940.*

*   *   *

WHEN DEMOCRACY THRIVES

Democracy can thrive only when it enlists the devotion of those whom Lincoln called the common people. Democracy can hold that devotion only when it adequately respects their dignity by so ordering society as to assure to the masses of men and women reasonable security and hope for themselves and for their children.—*Talk to the nation, July 19, 1940.*

DEMOCRACY IS A LIVING THING

Democracy is not just a word, to be shouted at political rallies and then put back into the dictionary after election day.

The service of democracy must be something much more than mere lip-service.

It is a living thing—a human thing—compounded of brains and muscles and heart and soul. The service of democracy is the birth-right of every citizen, the white and the colored; the Protestant, the Catholic, the Jew; the sons and daughters of every country in the world, who make up the people of this land. Democracy is every man and woman who loves freedom and serves the cause of freedom.—*Campaign address, Nov. 4, 1940.*

*   *   *

FOUNDATIONS OF A DEMOCRACY

There is nothing mysterious about the foundations of a healthy and strong democracy. The basic things expected by our people of their political and economic systems are simple. They are:

Equality of opportunity for youth and for others.

Jobs for those who can work.

Security for those who need it.

The ending of special privilege for the few.

The preservation of civil liberties for all.

The enjoyment of the fruits of scientific progress in a wider and constantly rising standard of living.—*Message to Congress, Jan. 6, 1941.*

*   *   *

DEMOCRACY CANNOT DIE!

There are men who believe that democracy, as a form of government and a frame of life, is limited or measured by a kind of mystical or artificial fate—that, for some unexplained reasons, tyranny and slavery have become the surging wave of the future and that freedom is an ebbing tide.

But we Americans know that this is not true. No, democracy is not dying.

We know it because we have seen it revive—and grow. We know it cannot die—because it is built on the unhampered initiative of individual men and women joined together in a common enterprise—an enterprise undertaken and carried through by the free expression of a free majority. We know it because democracy alone, of all forms of government, enlists the full force of men's enlightened will. We know it because democracy alone has constructed an unlimited civilization capable of infinite progress in the improvement of human life.

We know it because, if we look below the surface, we sense it still spreading on every continent; for it is the most humane, the most advanced and in the end the most unconquerable of all forms of human society.

The democratic aspiration is no mere recent phase in human history. It is human history.—*Third Inaugural Address, Jan. 20, 1941.*

*   *   *

AN ECONOMIC BILL OF RIGHTS

We have accepted, so to speak, a second bill of rights under which a new basis of security and prosperity can be established for all, regardless of station, race or creed. Among these are:

The right to a useful and remunerative job in the industries or shops or farms or mines of the nation.

The right of every farmer to raise and sell his products at a return which will give him and his family a decent living.

The right of every business man, large and small, to trade in an atmosphere of freedom from unfair competition and domination by monopolies at home or abroad.

The right of every family to a decent home.

The right to adequate medical care and the opportunity to achieve and enjoy good health.

The right to adequate protection from the economic fears of old age, sickness, accident and unemployment.

The right to a good education.—*Message to Congress, Jan. 11, 1944.*

*   *   *

AGAINST ANTI-SEMITISM

Some of the sources of anti-Semitism in this country were created to serve Hitler's purpose. Let every American look to his own mind and actions so that while we defeat Hitler's armies we also defeat his poisonous propaganda. Whoever condones or participates in anti-Semitism plays Hitler's game. There is no place in the lives or thoughts of true Americans for anti-Semitism.—*Letter to Rabbi Stephen S. Wise, Feb. 12, 1944.*

*   *   *

THE RIGHT TO VOTE

The right to vote must be open to our citizens irrespective of race, color or creed, without tax or artificial restriction of any kind. The sooner we get to that basis of political equality, the better it will be for the country as a whole.—*Address to Democratic Party workers, Oct. 5, 1944.*

THE STORY THE CAMERA TELLS

The best pictures relating
to F.D.R.'s life and works,
totalling (with end-leaves,
frontispiece, jacket and
textual illustrations) 200.

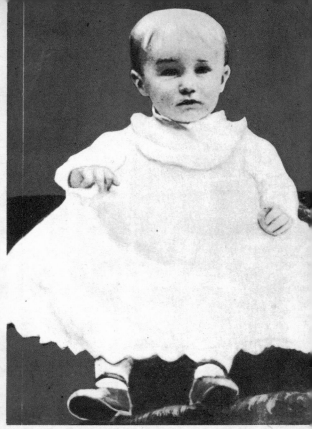

HE WAS BORN JANUARY 30, 1882, AT THE ANCESTRAL ESTATE OF HIS FATHER, JAMES ROOSEVELT, AT HYDE PARK, N. Y.

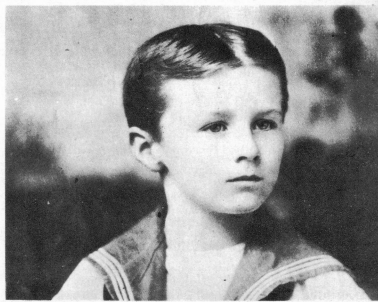

HIS ANCESTORS GOT THEIR WEALTH FROM SHIPPING, AND IN CHILDHOOD HIS AMBITIONS CENTERED AROUND THE NAVY.

HE IS SHOWN WITH HIS FATHER, WHO DIED IN 1901, WHEN FRANKLIN WAS A HARVARD STUDENT AND (r.) ON THE VARSITY.

ELEANOR ROOSEVELT, SHOWN (r.) WITH HER FATHER AND BROTHERS, WAS A NIECE OF T.R., A COUSIN OF HER HUSBAND.

THEY BECAME ENGAGED WHILE HE WAS A HARVARD UNDERGRADUATE, WERE MARRIED ON ST. PATRICK'S DAY, 1905.

HE VISITED LONDON to synchronize U. S. naval efforts with those of Great Britain. He met and began his friendship with Winston Churchill.

IN HIS FIRST U. S. POST, Assistant Secretary of the Navy, he roused defense workers . . .

HE BECAME A POPULAR FIGURE at service football games and in Washington socialdom, was boomed as a gubernatorial prospect.

HE DECLINED the New York governorship nomination then, remained to help his chief, Josephus Daniels (c.) put the Navy on a peacetime basis. In this picture he (straw hat) is attending demobilization of World War I's women Marines and Waves.

IN A RARE PHOTO OF THE TWO GREAT WAR PRESIDENTS, ASST. NAVY SECTY. F. D. ROOSEVELT (A) STANDS LOOKING WITH EVIDENT ADMIRATION AT PRESIDENT WOODROW WILSON (B) AT A REVIEW OF MARINES IN WASHINGTON, AUG. 12, 1919.

MR. ROOSEVELT WITH DAUGHTER ANNA AT CAMPOBELLO, IN 1920, WHEN HE BECAME A VICE PRESIDENTIAL NOMINEE.

HE LOVED HUNTING AND MOST OUTDOOR SPORTS.

In 1920, F.D.R. refused a second time to run for governor of New York and then, out of a clear sky was named the Democratic Vice Presidential candidate. He resigned his Navy post and campaigned for Cox (right), so ably as to impress himself on many in the party as the one who did not have to lean on the grand old name of Roosevelt to have a big future. The voters rejected the Wilsonian concept of a new world for which Cox and Roosevelt fought, and F.D.R. retired to private life as vice president of a bonding concern and resumed law practice. He enjoyed anew, with his five children, the active life outdoors that he loved. One day at the family summer home at Campobello, New Brunswick, he took a plunge in the cold bay. That night he had chills. Next day he had fever. Three days later he was paralyzed from the waist down, victim of infantile paralysis at 39. For months he was bedfast. A year later he could move only in a wheel chair or on crutches. It was assumed his professional and political life were over. Those who so assumed didn't know him.

AT WARM SPRINGS, GA., in 1924, Mr. Roosevelt found ways and means of re-conditioning his polio-affected legs.

HE SPENT HOURS SWIMMING, TO EXERCISE HIS LEGS.

HE RODE HORSEBACK OVER THE COUNTRYSIDE.

AND STRONG AGAIN, BEGAN TO BE INCREASINGLY ACTIVE.

1924 WAS THE CRUCIAL YEAR in F.D.R.'s life. Four years before, he had made his first venture into high politics and as Cox's Vice Presidential running mate, had been defeated. Struck down in the prime of life by infantile paralysis, he had endured two years of invalidism and knew that he would not walk again without crutches or braces. Engaging in national affairs anew meant taxing himself physically to the utmost. He had given himself unsparingly in an attempt to gain the 1924 Democratic Presidential nomination for Alfred E. Smith, New York's progressive governor, and had met another defeat: John W. Davis, a Wall Street lawyer, had been nominated instead. He could settle down comfortably as lawyer and land squire, enjoy life and perhaps prolong it. But Franklin D. Roosevelt was a born leader who could never retire. Once Charles Michelson asked him, "How on earth did you accumulate so much definite knowledge of so many things," and F.D.R. replied, with no suggestion of self-pity, "You fellows with two good legs spend your time playing golf or such things. I have to get my exercise out of a book." Yet the knowledge he had gained in his illness had not all come out of books. It had come out of his heart and his thinking over of the ills of the human and the social body. It had come out of his determination that there must be a shift in the power ruling the lives of the common man in America.

He chose to remain in politics, come what may. In a republic, change could come only through political processes. He supported John W. Davis' campaign, which started with a speech at Roosevelt's Hyde Park, where this photo, showing l. to r.: Lieut. Gov. George R. Nunn, F.D.R., Davis, and Governor Alfred E. Smith, was made.

In the next four years, he became an increasingly formidable figure in New York State and in 1928, when he nominated Smith for the Presidency as the "Happy Warrior," he was the obvious choice to head the ticket in New York and try to insure Smith's carrying the State. Smith lost the State and the election, but Roosevelt won the governorship. His opponent was Albert Ottinger, the encumbent Republican State attorney-general, who had made enemies within his own party. In important Erie county, a bi-partisan deal swung votes to Roosevelt for governor and to the Republican candidate for attorney-general. Roosevelt was able to carry the State by the narrow margin of 26,064. By that margin F.D.R. won the place of leading contender for the national nomination in 1932.

SPEAKING AT WARM SPRINGS (ABOVE), HE REPAIRED DAMAGE DONE TO PARTY LINES IN THE SOUTH IN 1928 CAMPAIGN.

A "BRAIN TRUST," including Judge Sam Rosenman (l.) and Herbert Lehman (c.), N. Y. banker, helped him with a program for the "Forgotten Man" that brought liberals to the support of his Presidential aspirations.

HE ATTRACTED many devoted aides like Marguerite LeHand (r.), who remained at his side through most of his public career as his secretary. He made her a beneficiary in his will, but she predeceased him a year.

IN 1930 F.D.R. was first Democrat since Civil War to carry both Gotham and Upstate New York.

WHEN 1932 CAME that made him a No. 1 choice to many party workers over Al Smith, whom he had nominated (above) in 1928.

JAMES A. FARLEY (L.) AND LOUIS M. HOWE (R.), HIS CHIEF POLITICAL LIEUTENANTS, LINED UP ALL THE SUPPORT HE NEEDED.

AS A PRESIDENTIAL CANDIDATE IN 1932, HE DID THE USUAL THINGS CANDIDATES DO: HE FISHED (AND LIKED IT);

HE BECAME AN HONORARY INDIAN;

HE GOT THE BEST ADVISORS. BARNEY BARUCH WAS ONE.

HE SHOWED HE LIKED COMMON FOOD.

HE GOT PRACTICAL POINTERS FROM WILSON'S E. H. HOUSE

THE NOMINATION WON, HE SHATTERED PRECEDENT TO FLY TO CHICAGO TO ACCEPT PARTY LEADERSHIP IMMEDIATELY.

L. to r.: WILL ROGERS, JIM FARLEY, W. G. McADOO, JAMES ROOSEVELT AND F.D.R. HIMSELF, FACING CONVENTION WHERE AFTER ENJOYING ROGERS' WISECRACKING, HE DECLARED, "I PLEDGE YOU, I PLEDGE MYSELF, A NEW DEAL."

HE WENT AMONG THE COMMON MEN, KNOWING AND SPEAKING THEIR LANGUAGE, AND THEY MADE HIM THEIR LEADER.

CHICAGO'S MAYOR CERMAK, FATALLY SHOT BY A BULLET INTENDED FOR F.D.R.—A FAMOUS PHOTO BY SAMMY SCHULMAN.

WHAT WOULD HAVE HAPPENED to the world subsequently if an assassin's bullet had found its mark in 1933 is a fascinating question. An eye-witness story of the attempt to assassinate F. D. R. in Miami is told by Sammy Schulman of INP:

"The newspapermen met Vincent Astor's yacht as it came into Miami, bringing Roosevelt from his pre-inauguration cruise. He called them aboard to tell them there had been a slight change in plans. The mayor of Miami, who had also come aboard, had asked him to say a few words to the people gathered in Bay Front Park.

"Roosevelt told the reporters that there wouldn't be anything to the speech. When he gave them a little dope on his fishing trip and his immediate plans, he urged them to go ahead and write their stories.

"All the boys except one took his tip and went off to work, but I decided to go to the Park. The mayor had a big line-up of cars at the pier to carry the President's party. I got in one.

"Our line of cars pulled into the Park on a narrow road that curved around in front of a band shell. While the other cars stopped, the Roosevelt car, which was a big open job, rolled on until it was directly in front of the shell. He hoisted himself up on the folded top behind the back seat, to speak.

"As the speech ended, I climbed down from the bandstand where I had been making some shots. I had seen Mayor Cermak climb down from the same stand and walk over to Roosevelt's car to chat with him for a moment. As I walked over to Cermak, Roosevelt slid down on the back seat again. The chauffeur of the Roosevelt car started its engine.

" 'Hello, Mr. Mayor,' I said to Cermak. 'Haven't seen you since the Congress Hotel.'

" 'Hello, boy,' Big Tony said. He talked about Chicago for a moment.

"Five sharp shots rose above the noise of the crowd, and I turned away from Cermak toward the direction of the noise. 'Sounds like Chicago, Mr. Mayor,' I said.

"Just as I said it a woman screamed and there was the crash of a tumbling chair. A heavy body hit me. It was Cermak. He hit the ground at my feet, gurgling. 'The President—get him away.'

"In the next few seconds. Gus Gennerich, Roosevelt's bodyguard, threw himself into the back of the car and pressed Roosevelt back against the seat, while he ordered the driver to go on. The car jerked forward, then stopped at Roosevelt's order.

"Cermak was still on the ground, looking up at me with hurt and unbelieving eyes. I yelled to Bob Clark, of the Secret Service.

"Clark called to L. L. Lee, the City Manager of Miami. They stooped quickly and pulled Cermak to his feet. He swayed back and forth, a red smear creeping around his white shirt, just above his belt. I had to shoot the picture quicker than I ever shot one, but I made it as they staggered toward the car.

"The crowd knew now and panic set in. I heard Roosevelt cry out, 'I'm all right,' as Cermak was lifted in beside him. A cop on the Roosevelt running board bellowed, 'Jackson Memorial Hospital,' and the car shot away as Roosevelt put his arm around Cermak to hold him upright on the seat."

HERBERT HOOVER (L.) AND F.D.R. LEAVE WHITE HOUSE, MARCH 4, 1933, FOR LATTER'S INAUGURATION, AMID A CRISIS.

AS NEW PRESIDENT SPOKE AT THE INAUGURATION, PAPERS WERE PREPARED FOR HIS SIGNATURE, SUSPENDING BANKING.

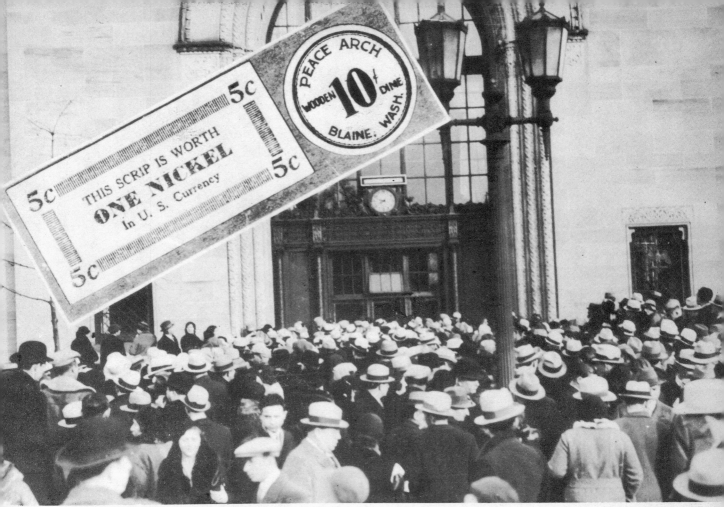

U. S. HAD BEEN SINKING INTO DEEP DEPRESSION FOR 3 YEARS. RUNS CLOSED BANKS, MADE SCRIPT-BARTER NECESSARY.

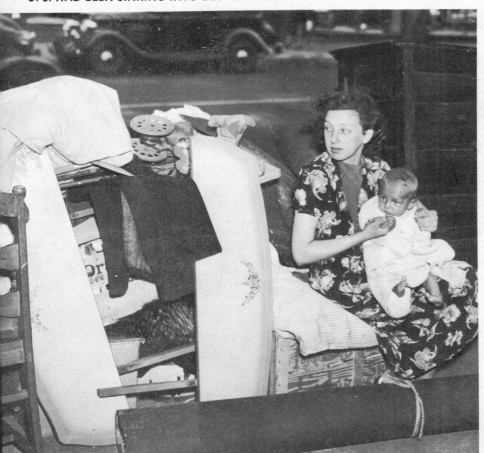

HUNDREDS OF THOUSANDS HAD BEEN MADE HOMELESS AND JOBLESS MIGRANTS ALL OVER WORLD'S RICHEST COUNTRY.

HE TOLD CONGRESS HIS PROGRAM FOR BATTLING THE CRISIS WITH REFORM. IT GAVE HIM UNPRECEDENTED POWERS.

IRST BEER, then liquor came back, with Congress and the ates enacting the necessary repeal legislation in record time.

USING RADIO regularly for "fireside chats," he rebuilt the confidence of common men in the U. S. government.

NO HEAD OF STATE IN HISTORY EVER CARRIED ON SUCH FRANK RELATIONS WITH THE PRESS. HE IS SEEN BEING QUIZZED.

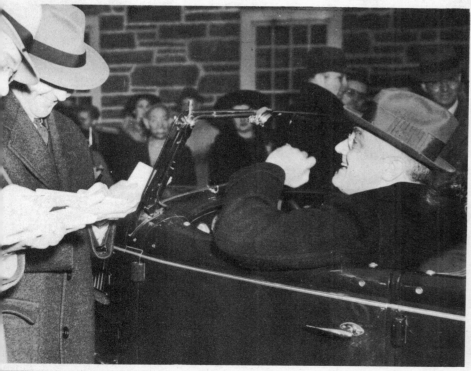

OLLAR REVALUED AT 59.06, GOLD PUT AT $35 AN OUNCE; STABILIZATION FUND SET UP

THIS IS F.D.R. in 1934, a little grayer, but cheerful and confident in the face of the fact that opponents of the New Deal are operating more openly now. Such actions as devaluing the dollar had ended his honeymoon with his party, too, but he was gaining supporters from other parties.

THIS WAS A PICTURE SOME PERSONS GOT OF WPA, WHICH PROVIDED OCCUPATIONS AND LIVELIHOOD FOR MILLIONS

BUT IT WAS NO JOKE TO OTHERS, WHOM WPA HAD HELPED, AND THEY FOUGHT FOR ITS PERMANENT CONTINUANCE

PRESIDENT ROOSEVELT understood that a sound national economy could not be founded on a dole. He said, "Continued dependence upon relief induces a spiritual and moral disintegration fundamentally destructive to the national fibre." He also said, "Some of these gentlemen tell me that a dole would be more economical than work relief. That is true. But . . . in this business of relief we are dealing with properly self-respecting Americans to whom a dole outrages every instinct of individual independence."

F.D.R. sought a planned economy in which there would be maximum employment with guaranteed annual wages and social security measures that would make doles unnecessary. Starting steps in that direction were the National Recovery Administration, under the driving, explosive Hugh Johnson (l.) which the still conservative Supreme Court found unconstitutional, and the Social Security Act, which became a law in 1935. Though the NRA label passed, the NRA's stamp remained on some sound business principles. The Social Security Act provides for old-age pensions, unemployment compensation, health and rehabilitation aid. It is an example of Roosevelt leadership in the same days in which WPA, CCC and such were termed "waste."

BUT THE CCC WAS A FOE OF WASTE: IT WENT INTO FORESTS, INTO DROUTH-DEVASTATED AREAS, PLANTING, CONSERVING.

HUNDREDS OF THOUSANDS OF BARREN ACRES BECAME GREEN AND PRODUCTIVE AGAIN, TO CREATE NEW WEALTH.

SCHOOLS

TRAINED MEN

HOMES FOR THE AGED

BRIDGES

HOSPITALS

THE PWA "BOONDOGGLED SOME," BUT IT ALSO DID MANY MORE LASTING THINGS—THINGS THAT YOU SEE NOW.

MUCH WATER flowed over the dam in the controversy over the Tennessee Valley Authority, which was created in 1933 and under F.D.R.'s pushing, swiftly began to develop and transform a large part of the neglected South. When the controversy was over the TVA Norris Dam (above) and others poured national resources and wealth into channels that spread them far and wide into factories, farms and homes. F.D.R. planned TVA's for other valleys at war's end.

BY 1935, THE VAST PUBLIC WORKS PROGRAM HAD "PRIMED THE PUMP" OF GOOD TIMES. ABOVE: A DRAINAGE PROJECT.

F.D.R. could speak, smilingly, of an "impossible task" accomplished by national co-operation.

OTHER COUNTRIES were still deep in depression. Here factories were (above) recalling unemployed to new jobs by the thousands.

MRS. ROOSEVELT'S OPENNESS, INFORMALITY, FRIENDLINESS, GAVE THE NATION A NEW CONCEPT OF A "FIRST LADY."

SHE SUBBED FOR FDR ON MANY PUBLIC OCCASIONS.

SHE WAS HIS EYES AND EARS AMONG THE COMMON MEN.

THE CHILDREN MADE NEWS: ANNA WAS DIVORCED, REWED.

LAWYER F. D., JR., WROTE POPULAR SONGS, MARRIED A DUPONT.

JAMES SOLD INSURANCE, PRODUCED MOVIES.
HIS MOTHER ACTED IN ONE OF HIS PICTURES.

ELLIOTT BROADCAST FOR PAY, BECAME A RADIO EXECUTIVE.

JOHN MARRIED, WORKED IN A BOSTON STORE.

IT COULDN'T have happened anywhere else—a head of state being lampooned on the stage, as F.D.R. was in a Broadway hit musical show, *I'd Rather Be Right*. He loved the wisecracks in it. He never made any attempt to restrain mimicry of himself or family on either stage or screen, and saw himself depicted in *Yankee Doodle Dandy* and other movies.

GEORGE M. COHAN AS FRANKLIN D. ROOSEVELT IN *I'D RATHER BE RIGHT*. THE WOMAN IS SUPPOSED TO BE MRS. R.

THE FATES: ' This day we fashion destiny. Our web of fate we spin.'

—London Daily Sketch

—New York Mirror

HE WAS AS AMUSED AS THE PUBLIC BY MANY OF THE CARTOONS ABOUT HIM AND ASKED ARTISTS FOR THE ORIGINALS.

© King Features Syndicate

HE REQUESTED "BRINGING UP FATHER" STRIPS BY GEORGE McMANUS IN WHICH HE APPEARED AS A CHARACTER.

MOST UNCHANGING OF F.D.R.'S FOREIGN POLICIES WAS GOOD NEIGHBORLINESS IN THE AMERICAS. HE WENT TO MEXICO . . .

. . . AND HE VISITED BRAZIL AND THROUGHOUT THE WESTERN HEMISPHERE, TO BUILD UP HEMISPHERIC SOLIDARITY.

HE MAINTAINED NO DISTINCTIONS BETWEEN AMERICANS BECAUSE OF RACE OR COLOR. HE HONORED MANY NEGROES.

COLOR DISCRIMINATION IN THE NAVY OFFICIALLY ENDED. NEGRO SPOKESMEN LIKENED MR. ROOSEVELT TO LINCOLN.

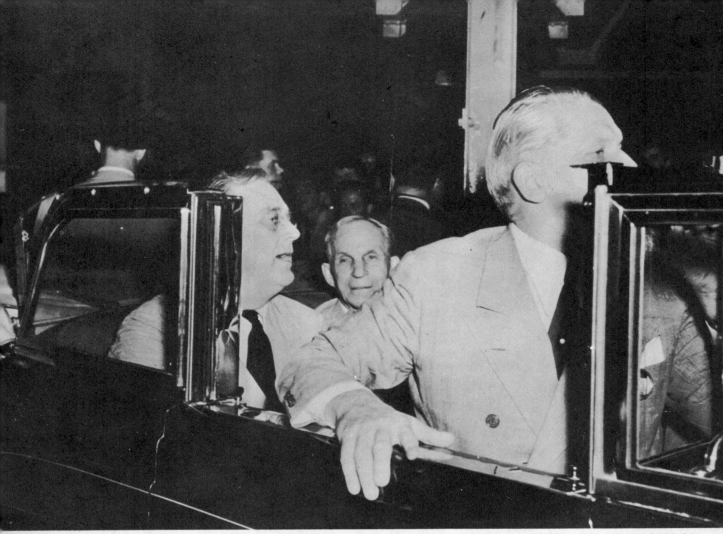

UNDER F.D.R., THE GOVERNMENT BECAME A PARTNER IN BUSINESS. HE IS SEEN WITH NO. 1 INDUSTRIALIST, HENRY FORD (c).

UNIONS ATTAINED great influence in his administration William Green (c.), president of A. F. of L. is shown at his side here.

MRS. ROOSEVELT, shown here with Sidney Hillman (c.) and Philip Murray, C.I.O. leaders, maintained close touch with labor movements, proved a helpful friend of unions and herself joined one (the Newspaper Guild).

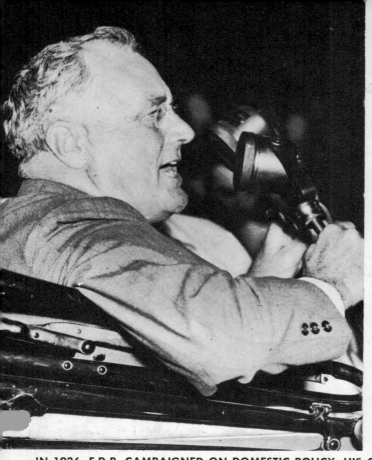

IN 1936, F.D.R. CAMPAIGNED ON DOMESTIC POLICY. HIS OPPONENT WAS GOV. ALF. LANDON (ARROW) OF KANSAS.

THE NATION APPROVED THE POLICY TO THE EXTENT THAT F.D.R. AND GARNER CARRIED ALL EXCEPT TWO STATES.

D. ACTS FOR WORLD PEACE, CURB ON NAZIS

WASHINGTON.—President Roosevelt today outlines part U. S. will play in maintaining peace of Europe. Statement looked upon as friendly warning to Hitler that U. S. is prepared to stand by France and Great Britain in opposing Germany's armament plans.

ROME—Premier Mussolini sends personal warning to Chancellor Hitler to moderate his views on Germany's rearmament and adopt a conciliatory attitude toward the British disarmament...

WHEN HITLER, HAVING CONQUERED GERMANY, BEGAN TO RAISE HIS MAILED FIST AT THE REST OF EUROPE . . .

Roosevelt Outlines Arms Policy Today

WASHINGTON, May 15 (US).—President Roosevelt will issue a momentous statement tomorrow outlining his views on disarmament and the part which the Administration is willing to play in maintaining the peace of Europe.

Clothing the forthcoming declaration in strictest secrecy, friends of the President described it as an American "Monroe Doctrine" towards Europe.

The fact that the administration's position will be stated to-morrow by the friendly warning to Chancellor Hitler of the...

PRESIDENT ROOSEVELT SPOKE OUT CLEARLY IN WARNING, WHILE OTHER HEADS OF STATES KEPT THEIR PEACE.

President Roosevelt makes it plain what is ahead, in his historic "Quarantine" speech:

"Without a declaration of war and without warning or justification of any kind, civilians, including vast numbers of women and children, are being ruthlessly murdered with bombs from the air. In times of so-called peace, ships are being attacked and sunk by submarines without cause or notice. Nations are fomenting and taking sides in civil warfare in nations that have never done them any harm. Nations claiming freedom for themselves deny it to others.

"Innocent peoples, innocent nations, are being cruelly sacrificed to a greed for power and supremacy which is devoid of all sense of justice and humane considerations . . .

"If those things come to pass in other parts of the world, let no one imagine that America will escape, that America may expect mercy, that this Western Hemisphere will not be attacked and that it will continue tranquilly and peacefully to carry on the ethics and the arts of civilization.

"If those days come 'there will be no safety by arms, no help from authority, no answer in science. The storm will rage till every flower of culture is trampled and all human beings are leveled in a vast chaos.'

"If those days are not to come to pass—if we are to have a world in which we can breathe freely and live in amity without fear—the peace-loving nations must make a concerted effort to uphold laws and principles on which alone peace can rest secure."

*Japan had invaded China, and European powers were active partisans in the Spanish Civil War.

UNDER A CANOPY, BEFORE A CHICAGO OPEN-AIR MEETING, OCT. 5, 1937, F.D.R. GIVES HIS BEST-REMEMBERED SPEECH.

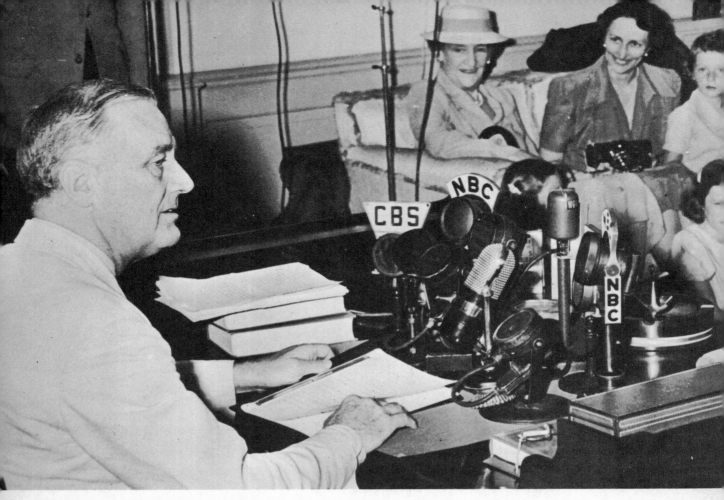

F.D.R. SPOKE on familiar terms to the world; he was the first U. S. President whose speeches were regularly carried on foreign networks. President Roosevelt saw much of the world in person; the world and its great came to him also. Above: Crown Princess Martha of Norway (hatless) enjoys a Presidential talk to the nation while a White House guest. In 1939, Britain's queen (in front, below) and king (rear) came to visit the Roosevelts and F.D.R. himself drove them around.

THE SIGNIFICANCE OF THE MEETINGS OF MUSSOLINI AND HITLER, OF JAPANESE EMISSARIES WITH THE REICHSFUEHRER . . .

. . . WERE NOT LOST UPON F.D.R. HE SAW HITLER AS THE ARCH-LEADER OF ALL THE WORLD'S ENEMIES OF DEMOCRACY.

New F.D. Plea Asks Hitler to Avert Disaster

ALL THE DIPLOMATIC MIGHT that F.D.R. summoned in 1939 proved ineffective against Hitler, who was determined upon war. He sought pledges of non-aggression by Germany and Italy against Poland, France, Denmark, Holland, Belgium, Russia and 24 other states for ten years, promising in return a world conference for solving problems between "haves" and "have-nots." But instead Germany made a 10-year non-aggression pact with Russia. Hitler ordered Poland invaded.

F.D. Sees World War, Asks Militia Control

Americas Are Untouchable, F.D.R. Warns

"No individual, no group, can clearly foretell the future. As long, however, as a possibility exists that not one continent or two continents but all continents may become involved in a world-wide war, reasonable precaution demands that American defense be made more certain."
—From President Roosevelt's message yesterday.

Welles Going Abroad To Hold Peace Talks

F.D. Reminds Hitler Of Pledges He Broke

50,000 WAR PLANES DEMANDED BY F.D.R.

F.D. TO CALL FOR FORCED TRAINING OF EVERY YOUTH

Roosevelt Feels U.S. Can't Risk Fleet Equality

F.D. to Demand Congress Speed Big Defense Sum

U.S. GIVES ENGLAND 50 DESTROYERS IN SWAP FOR 8 BASES

PREACHERS PRAISE, ATTACK PRESIDENT

Gun Sale OK'd by Senate; F.D. Asks War Relief Fund

U.S. DRIVE FOR PEACE OPENED ON 3 FRONTS

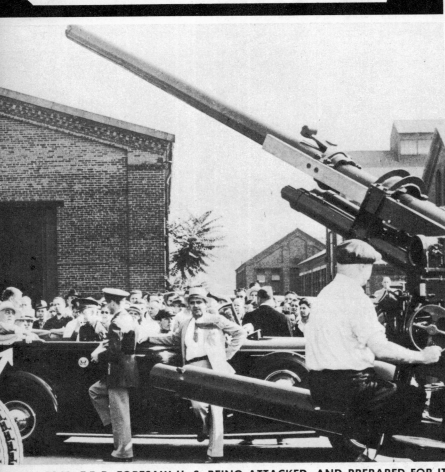

IN 1940, F.D.R. FORESAW U.S. BEING ATTACKED, AND PREPARED FOR IT; BUT COULD NOT IGNORE THE FACT MANY IN THE NATION STILL BELIEVED WAR COULD BE AVERTED. THE ISSUE MADE THE 1940 CAMPAIGN A WARM ONE.

By **WALTER FITZMAURICE**.

WASHINGTON, April 13 (INS). — President Roosevelt branding Germany's invasion of Scandinavia unlawful," tonight rejected in effect the Reich's claim that the attack constituted legal reprisal for the British mining of Norwegian waters.

With Denmark in subjugation and the Allies bolstering Norway's struggle, the President condemned last Tuesday's blitzrieg as naked "aggression."

ON ROSTRUM, THROUGH PRESS, F.D.R. WARNED.

WITH THE LOW COUNTRIES and France invaded and conquered by aerial blitzkrieg, President Roosevelt declared the waters of the Atlantic no longer protected the U. S.; that the nation must prepare. But in asking Congress for five billion dollars for defenses, he said, "That we are opposed to war is well known not only to every American but to every government in the world. We will not use our arms in a war of aggression." The day after the climactic day of the Battle of Britain, when the R.A.F. bombed out an invasion attempt (Sept. 16, 1940), he signed the Selective Service Act and set Oct. 16 as the registration day when Secretary of War Stimson (blindfolded) would draw the first numbers and start the machinery of training millions of American men for war. The President had brought two life-long Republicans into his Cabinet to be the Secretaries of War and Navy. The latter, Frank Knox, had been Landon's running-mate against F.D.R. in 1936. In England, that dark October, Churchill had become premier as head of a coalition government.

WENDELL WILLKIE, SHOWN WITH ELLIOTT ROOSEVELT, WHO HIMSELF HAD QUESTIONED SOME NEW DEAL POLICIES, DID NOT DIFFER BASICALLY WITH F.D.R. ON FOREIGN STATECRAFT, AND BASED HIS CAMPAIGN ON DOMESTIC ISSUES.

WITH A NEW VICE PRESIDENTIAL RUNNING MATE, HENRY WALLACE (L.), F.D.R. WON AN UNPRECEDENTED 3RD TERM.

THE PRESIDENT RETURNS FROM AN INSPECTION TRIP TO BARRIERS TO INVASION IN WEST INDIES AND THE CARIBBEAN. HIS SWAP OF DESTROYERS TO GREAT BRITAIN IN 1940 MADE POSSIBLE THIS PROTECTION AGAINST GERMAN DESIGNS.

FIGURATIVE neutrality of U. S. ended early in 1941. F.D.R. decided U. S. could no longer stand by while Hitler crushed both Russia and Britain. Congress implemented the supplying of billions in supplies to the Nazi-beseiged nations, which had already begun, with the Lend-Lease Act. To insure efficient cooperation, F.D.R. took his staff to meet Churchill and his staff on the high seas. Together, when their military plans had been laid, they wrote a plan for the peace they hoped for after war.

The San Francisco Conference and its preparatory predecessor, the Dumbarton Oaks Conference, both had their foundations resting upon the so-called Atlantic Charter:

The President of the United States of America and the Prime Minister, Mr. Churchill, representing His Majesty's Government in the United Kingdom, being met together, deem it right to make known certain common principles in the national policies of their respective countries on which they base their hopes for a better future for the world.

First, their countries seek no aggrandizement, territorial or other;

Second, they desire to see no territorial changes that do not accord with the freely expressed wishes of the peoples concerned;

Third, they respect the right of all peoples to choose the form of government under which they will live; and they wish to see sovereign rights and self-government restored to those who have been forcibly deprived of them;

Fourth, they will endeavor, with due respect for their existing obligations, to further the enjoyment of all States, great or small, victor or vanquished, of access, on equal terms, to the trade and to the raw materials of the world which are needed for their economic prosperity;

Fifth, they desire to bring about the fullest collaboration between all nations in the economic field with the object of securing, for all, improved labor standards, economic adjustment and social security.

Sixth, after the final destruction of the Nazi tyranny, they hope to see established a peace which will afford to all nations the means of dwelling in safety within their own boundaries, and which will afford assurance that all the men in all the lands may live out their lives in freedom from fear and want;

Seventh, such a peace should enable all men to traverse the high seas and oceans without hindrance;

Eighth, they believe that all the nations of the world, for realistic as well as spiritual reasons, must come to the abandonment of the use of force. Since no future peace can be maintained if land, sea or air armaments continue to be employed by nations which threaten, or may threaten, aggression outside of their frontiers, they believe, pending the establishment of a wider and permanent system of general security, that the disarmament of such nations is essential.

They will likewise aid and encourage all other practicable measures which will lighten peace-loving peoples the crushing burden of armament.

Subsequently, after Yalta, Mr. Roosevelt commented:

It is true that the statement of principles of the Atlantic Charter does not provide rules of easy application to each and every one of this war-torn world tangled situations. But it is a good and useful thing—it is an essential thing—to have principles toward which we can aim.

MRS. ROOSEVELT, THE PRESIDENT, AND BODYGUARD THOMAS QUALTERS, ON AN UNOFFICIAL VISIT TO NEW YORK IN 1941. ONLY THOSE CLOSEST TO HIM EVER REALIZED HOW MUCH OF HIS GREATNESS FRANKLIN OWED TO ELEANOR ROOSEVELT.

Congress, April 2, 1917

"The world must be made safe for democracy."

Woodrow Wilson

Arlington National Cemetery
November 11, 1941

"*They did not die to make the world safe...for five years, or ten, or maybe twenty. They died to make it safe. And if, by some fault of ours who lived beyond the war, its safety has again been threatened, then the obligation and the duty are ours.*"—The President.

Congress, Dec. 8, 1941

"*I ask that the Congress declare that since the unprovoked and dastardly attack by Japan...a state of war has existed between the United States and the Japanese Empire.*"

Franklin D. Roosevelt

The President's Call to War

TO THE CONGRESS OF THE UNITED STATES:

YESTERDAY, DECEMBER 7, 1941,—a date which will live in infamy—the United States of America was suddenly and deliberately attacked by naval and air forces of the Empire of Japan.

The United States was at peace with that nation and, at the solicitation of Japan, was still in conversation with its Government and its Emperor looking toward the maintenance of peace in the Pacific.

Indeed, one hour after Japanese air squadrons had commenced bombing in Oahu, the Japanese Ambassador to the United States and his colleague delivered to the Secretary of State a formal reply to a recent American message. While this reply that it seemed useless to the existing diplomatic negotiations, it contained war or armed attack.

It will be recorded that from Japan makes it obvious deliberately planned many During the intervening ment has states by or continued

WILSON, 1917 able to believe be done subscribe ized nation

The attack

een lo eported rancisco a

Yest aunch

Kong. Last nig Last ine Island Last Th island

1917: A American lives taken, i has stirred us very deeply

Japan has, therefore, undertaken a surprise offensive extending throughout the Pacific area. The facts of yesterday speak for themselves. The people of the United States have already formed their opinions and well understand the implications to the very life and safety of our nation.

As Commander-in-Chief of the Army and Navy

I have that all measures be taken for our defe remember character of the take us to over- rican hrough

TWIN RESOLUTIONS are the two Congressional acts which declared war officially against the German Government in 1917 and the Japanese Government in 1941. Senator Tom Connally, of Texas, Chairman of the Senate Foreign Relations Committee who yerday's viously er declara- pattern.

esolution

AS the Imperial ese Government has ed unprovoked acts inst the Government United herefore

Senate and resentatives of tes of America embled, that a state the United panese thus e United formally de President is and directed

panese ing the e of the termina- d by ited

ution

he recent acts rial German ts of war ment and the United States; d by the Senate and House representatives of the United States of America in Congress assembled, that the state of war between the United States and the Imperial German Government which has been thrust upon the United States is formally declared;

"And that the President be and he is hereby, authorised and directed to take immediate steps, not only to put the country in a thorough state of defense, but also to exert all of its power and employ all of its resources to carry on war against the Imperial German Government and to bring the

my l du Congress a recent of the Imperial German Government to be in fact nothing less than war against the Government and people of the United States; that it formally accept the status of belligerent which has thus been thrust upon it; and that it take immediate steps—not only to put the country in a more thorough state of defense but also to exert all its power and employ all its resources to bring the Government of the German Empire

THE WORLD BEHIND THE HEADLINES

11th-Hr. Plea Sent by F.D. to Japs' Emperor

By ROBERT G. NIXON.

WASHINGTON, Dec. 6 (INS).—President Roosevelt in a desperate last-hour attempt to avert outbreak of a major conflict in the Pacific, tonight addressed a personal message to Emperor Hirohito of Japan. The President's dramatic action came as the American Government was informed of Japanese preparation of an imminent invasion of Thailand, including heavy increases in troop shipments to Indo-China.

The State Department made the bare announcement that President Roosevelt was stepping into the situation through personal intercession with the Japanese Emperor. The contents of the message were not disclosed.

The President acted swiftly as every indication to the American Government was that Japan has troops in movement in Southern Indo-China for invasion of Thailand that may come at any hour.

Fleet Convoys Troopships

A last-minute diplomatic and military intelligence report to Washington late this afternoon stated, the State Department disclosed, that Japan already has sent a total of 125,000 troops into Indo-China and that Japanese convoys heavily escorted by units of the Japanese fleet have been seen off the southern point of Indo-China, speeding toward the Gulf of Siam.

The State Department asserted that of the total of 125,000 Japanese troops in the occupied Vichy colony, it is estimated 82,000 have already been landed in South Indo-China opposite Thailand and that there are an additional 25,000 Japanese troops in Northern Indo-China.

Another 18,000 Japanese troops, according to reports to the American Government, are on board 21 Japanese transports now in Camranh Bay, principal southern

Japs Mass Troops

Map showing China, Burma, Thailand, Indo-China, British Malaya, and Singapore with troop movements marked.

25,000 Jap Troops Concentrated in North Indo-China

18,000 Soldiers On Transports in Camranh Bay

67,000 Jap Soldiers Reported Here

Two Large Jap Convoys Seen Headed Toward Gulf of Siam

While Japan reportedly massed troops at strategic points, Singapore (A) was put on a state of mobilized readiness.

0   200
MILES

THE ENEMY HAD MADE THE CHOICE between peace and war. Now the President spoke to Congress and to the nation. We must fight. Congress declared war and the nation approved. It did not fully realize the task ahead: no nation had ever waged war before with so many and strong enemy nations.

REGISTRATION CERTIFICATE

This is to certify that in accordance with the
Selective Service Proclamation of the President of the United States

Franklin .... **Delano** .... **Roosevelt**
(First name) .... (Middle name) .... (Last name)

1600 Pennsylvania Ave., Washington,D.C.
(Place of residence)

(This will be identical with line 2 of the Registration Card)

has been duly registered this **27th** day of **April**, 19**42**

James H Hayes
(Signature of registrar)

Registrar for Local Board ..... **9** ..... **Washington,** ..... **D.C.**
(Number) .... (City or county) .... (State)

THE LAW REQUIRES YOU TO HAVE THIS CARD IN YOUR PERSONAL POSSESSION AT ALL TIMES

D. S. S. Form 2 .... 16—21631
(Revised 6/9/41)

(Registrant must sign here) *Franklin D Roosevelt*

WHEN DRAFT LAW WAS AMENDED IN 1942 TO TAKE IN OLDER PERSONS, F.D.R. HIMSELF HAD TO BECOME A REGISTRANT.

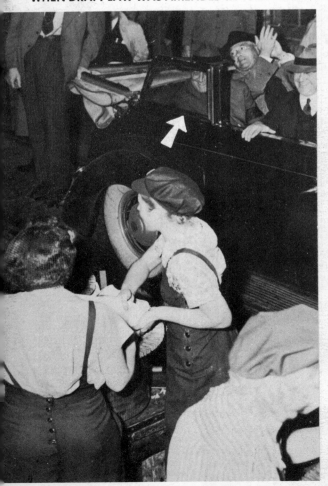

HE (ARROW) AND MRS. ROOSEVELT (R.) TOURED THE COUNTRY REPEATEDLY, SPURRING THE DOMESTIC WAR EFFORT.

ALL FOUR Roosevelt sons entered the service. John, shown (r.) with a fellow officer, joined the Navy as an ensign.

F.D., JR. (r., with his skipper), had taken pre-war training to be Navy officer.

ELLIOTT (l., with father overseas), rose to be a brigadier-general in Air Corps.

JIMMY, THE ELDEST, LEFT A WIFE AND CHILDREN AND OVERCAME ILL-HEALTH TO BE A MARINE FIELD-OFFICER (r.).

UNDER F.D.R. Washington took the place of both London and Geneva as centers of diplomacy. Here he presides at a conference of Pacific powers, in 1943, attended by Churchill (1), Canada's Premier King (2), Philippine President Quezon (3), and spokesmen of China, Australia, and New Zealand. As he devoted increasing attention to foreign affairs on defense plant tours (below, at Willow Run) and spent more time away from Washington. he incurred more reverses on the political front. Such as the reaction to his appointment of his old friend and political advisor, Edward P. Flynn of New York's party machine, to an ambassadorship Flynn wanted.

February 1, 1943.

Dear Ed:-

Reluctantly, I am complying with your request and have withdrawn your nomination from the Senate.

I wish you would come to see me today or tomorrow.

As ever yours,

Franklin D Roosevelt

Honorable Edward J. Flynn,
The Mayflower,
Washington, D. C.

F.D.R. (L.), CHURCHILL AND STALIN, AT TEHERAN, IRAN, WHERE THE "BIG THREE" HAD THEIR FIRST MEETING.

HE TRIED to be a peacemaker between Gens. Giraud (l.), who aided U. S. in African invasion, and DeGaulle (r.), French leader.

F.D.R. SMASHED more precedents late in 1943, when in his role of leader of the democracies, he flew to Teheran and Cairo. At the former he timed U. S. invasion of France with Russian drive on Germans from East, allocated the planes, guns and food necessary to supply the latter. At Cairo, he made working agreements with Chiang Kai-shek (below) on the war against Japan.

NOT ONE BUT SEVERAL FLEETS MORE POWERFUL THAN ANY OTHERS IN THE WORLD STRETCHED ACROSS THE PACIFIC. F.D.R. WENT TO HAWAII H.Q. TO CONFER WITH MacARTHUR (l.), LEAHY, AND NIMITZ (r.) ON CRUSHING JAPS WITH THEM.

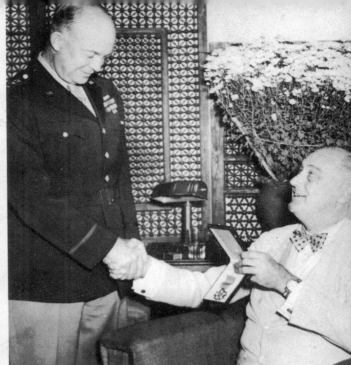

F.D.R. FUNCTIONED FAR MORE AS COMMANDER-IN-CHIEF THAN ANY PREDECESSOR SINCE ABE LINCOLN. LIKE LINCOLN, HE VISITED HIS COMMANDERS IN THE FIELD. L.: WITH MACARTHUR IN HAWAII; R. WITH EISENHOWER ABROAD.

ABOVE: (L. TO R.) HARRY HOPKINS, GEN. MARK CLARK, F.D.R., GEN. GEO. PATTON LUNCHING IN NORTH AFRICA.

HE WENT AMONG SOLDIERS IN THE PACIFIC AND CAME BACK, TIRED, TO WAGE A POLITICAL BATTLE WITH T. E. DEWEY.

HE EXPENDED FAILING STRENGTH TO MAKE HIS CAMPAIGN APPEAL TO HIS HOME STATE PEOPLE IN 1944 FACE-TO-FACE.

ELECTION NIGHT, 1944. HE IS THE PEOPLE'S CHOICE AGAIN.

CORDELL HULL (r.) RESIGNED FROM CABINET

EDWARD STETTINIUS (r., INTRODUCING A VISITOR) BECAME SECRETARY OF STATE. F.D.R.'s DAUGHTER ANNA IS AT LEFT.

A FEW DAYS after his fourth inauguration, President Roosevelt left for Yalta
(above), Russia, for the climax of his
epochal career in international statecraft.

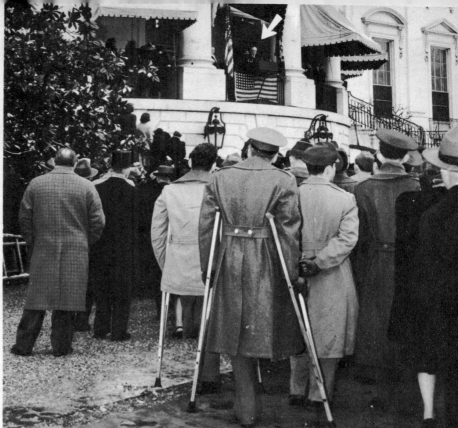

INCLEMENT WEATHER CONFINED INAUGURATION TO WHITE HOUSE.

L. to r.: BRITAIN'S WINSTON CHURCHILL, AMERICA'S FRANKLIN ROOSEVELT, RUSSIA'S JOSEPH STALIN POSE AT YALTA.

DIFFERENCES BETWEEN CHURCHILL (1) AND STALIN (2) ROSE AT YALTA. ROOSEVELT (3) HAD THE BALANCE OF POWER.

LEFT: MAISKY, OF RUSSIAN FOREIGN OFFICE, SPEAKS AN ASIDE TO STALIN; RIGHT: HOPKINS (1) SPEAKS TO F.D.R.

F.D.R. MET FIRST ONE, THEN OTHER, TO IRON OUT ISSUES OVER POLAND AND THREE VOTES FOR U.S.S.R. IN PEACE.

ON HIS WAY HOME FROM YALTA, HE MAPPED FINAL BLOWS FOR VICTORY WITH (l. to r.) LEAHY, KING AND MARSHALL.

BACK IN WASHINGTON, HE CONFERRED WITH DELEGATES TO SAN FRANCISCO, INTENT UPON INSURING THE PEACE, ALSO.

IT WAS PLAIN TO MANY WHO LISTENED TO HIS REPORT TO CONGRESS ON YALTA, THAT HIS HEALTH WAS FAILING.

HE BEGAN GAYLY, JOKING ABOUT ROOSEVELT TRAVELS, BUT SOON TIRED AND HIS VOICE WAVERED AND FALTERED.

FLASH   WASHN--FDR DEAD. INS WASHN 4/12/54???..

TXN17   BUN SUB FLASH
         WASHINGTON, APRIL 12--(INS)--THE WHITE HOUSE ANNOUNCED THIS AFTERNOON
THAT PRESIDENT ROOSEVELT IS DEAD.   MORE 548PPH

TXN18   BUN ADD FDR WASHN XX IS DEAD.
         THE PRESIDENT DIED AT WARM SPRINGS, GA.
         MORE 548PPH

TXN19   BUN ADD FDR WASH XX SPRINGS, GA.
         PRESIDENT ROOSEVELT SUCCUMBED TO A CEREBRAL HEMORRHAGE, IT WAS
ANNOUNCED BY STEPHEN EARLY, PRESIDENTIAL SECRETARY. VICE PRESIDENT HARRY
S. TRUMAN HAS BEEN NOTIFIED OF THE PRESIDENT'S DEATH AND IS ALREADY
PREPARING TO TAKE OVER THE OFFICE OF PRESIDENT.

Daily Mirror

3c In Suburbs
5c Elsewhere
In United States

2¢

FINAL 6 A.M. ★★★★

NEW YORK, FRIDAY, APRIL 13, 1945

F.D.R. DEAD

End Comes at Warm Springs; Truman Sworn as President

— Story on Page 3 —

IT SEEMED UNBELIEVABLE AT FIRST, BUT THERE IT WAS, IN THE PAPERS AND ON THE RADIO. THE NATION BOWED ITS HEAD.

HE WAS laughing just before he became unconscious. His secretary, Bill Hassett, had official papers freshly signed by F.D.R., which could not be blotted, spread out around the room, and apologized for delay he was causing the sketch artist by saying, "I'm waiting for my laundry to dry." The President laughed, then concentrated on more papers and made no other sound until he spoke his last words 15 or 20 minutes later. "I noticed as his face would turn partly away from me that he looked younger than the previous day," said the artist. "He looked strangely well." She did not complete her portrait and she has said that she won't. But a portrait she did in April 1943, hangs in a room of the White House.

MRS. ELIZABETH SHOUMATOFF WAS SKETCHING HIM. "WE'VE JUST ABOUT 15 MINUTES MORE TO WORK," HE SAID . . .

A MOMENT LATER, IN THIS COTTAGE, HE MURMURED, "I'VE GOT A TERRIFIC HEADACHE," AND PASSED TO THE HEREAFTER.

THE NATION is grieved, millions feeling a personal loss, but not alarmed. For as he becomes President, Harry S. Truman pledges himself to carry on the policies of Franklin Roosevelt.

THE BODY LEAVES WARM SPRINGS, GA., IN A HEARSE, AS THE WORLD, TOO, BESPEAKS ITS SENSE OF GREAT LOSS.

HE DIED WITH VICTORY AT HAND. OUR FLAG FLEW OVER THE RHINE (L.), GERMANS WERE SURRENDERING BY THOUSANDS.

JAPAN'S NAVY WAS FAST DISAPPEARING, AND OUR FLAG WAS ON OKINAWA, ONLY 300 MILES AWAY FROM TOKYO.

FROM THE RECORD

By Robert G. Nixon

As White House correspondent of International News Service, Mr. Nixon was one of three press association correspondents who accompanied Mr. Roosevelt in all his travels in F.D.R.'s last years. On many of the trips, no other reporters were along. The President took the trio into his confidence and gave them information "off the record" regarding his actions, plans and hopes.

CIRCUMSTANCES and a genius for dealing with them have given Franklin Delano Roosevelt† a contemporary ranking among the greatest figures in all world history. It is altogether likely that time and perspective will make this rating permanent.

There is no question of his right to a place with the greatest men of his own nation—Washington, Franklin, Jefferson and Lincoln.

Under his dynamic leadership, the American nation threw off the effects of a world wide economic depression that had created widespread unrest in the early Thirties, and instituted a vast program of social change designed to give those in the lower economic levels greater security, improved living and working conditions, and a larger share in the management of industry and business. No nation ever achieved greater success with such a program.

Then, in its greatest crisis since the Civil War, he led the nation through the years of the second World War against the combined forces of Fascist, Nazi and Bushido would-be world conquerers to the point where victory was certain. When he died, the United States had reached the position of the paramount power in the world and largely as a result of Mr. Roosevelt's initiative and foresight.

He was one of the first if not the first leader in a democracy to recognize and realize the danger from forces of evil gathering through the Thirties to launch attempted world conquest. He spoke out and denounced them when other leaders of States were still consorting with the Fascist leaders openly or were silent. He prepared as well as conservative public opinion and Congress would permit him, for the gathering storm by

revitalizing the American navy—the nation's first line of defense. He recognized the potent threat of air power before Germany first unleashed it with such devastating effect, and began preparations for this country's present dominant air forces.

In the dark days after Dunkirk, when Britain stood alone, he came to its aid with the startling innovation of Lend-Lease. He had already given England arms and ammunition to help stave off a German invasion after the little British army had been disarmed at Dunkirk. He sent Britain ships, planes, tanks and guns when the United States was still at peace, believing that if England fell, all civilization as the democratic world knew it, might disappear from the face of the earth. The knowledge that America was behind them, gave the valiant Britons greater courage to persevere against seemingly impossible odds.

In aiding Britain and, later, Russia to an extent that enabled each to stave off Nazi defeat and then, with the United States itself finally an active belligerent overseas, to destroy the German military juggernaut, Mr. Roosevelt had to make a choice of such momentous proportions as had never had been thrust upon an American President. The choice, of course, was whether to postpone a showdown with Japan in the Pacific or to give Britain and Russia the aid they needed to defeat Germany.

When the Japs made their sneak attack on Pearl Harbor, a large part of the United States fleet was in the Atlantic, protecting the supply line to Russia and to Britain. The Japs sank or damaged a large part of the force concentrated at Pearl Harbor. Consequently, for months there was no American naval force large enough to block Jap expansion through the Philippines, British colonies and Dutch East Indies into the biggest Pacific empire in history. The Japs in-

---

†The correct pronunciation of the name is Rō′zě-vĕlt.

vaded North America itself, in outer Alaskan islands.

Mr. Roosevelt calmed the nation's fears and rallied it to fight two widely separated major wars simultaneously—something no other nation in history had ever done successfully. Mighty fleets of ships upon which construction had been begun, at his urging, before the U. S. started waging the dual wars, eventually appeared upon the oceans to confront the enemy and drive his ships into home waters or sink them. Airplanes streamed out of American factories in numbers in excess of the wildest estimates of pre-war years. The United States brought into its armed services, trained and transported overseas, fully equipped, the largest expeditionary forces in history. Meanwhile its factories and farms also poured out hundreds of thousands of tons of supplies to enable Britain and Russia and dozens of smaller nations to combat the enemy. In all this the biggest individual driving force was Franklin Delano Roosevelt. He set the pace, he made the demands, and the nation kept and fulfilled them.

Mr. Roosevelt exerted all this energy and made himself a large niche in history's hall of fame against odds that would have made many another man fail. For when in the prime of life, he had been stricken by a devastating illness that left him a cripple. During the last 24 years of his life, he could not take a step unaided.

THE early life of Franklin Delano Roosevelt was cut more to the pattern of George Washington and Thomas Jefferson than to that of Benjamin Franklin and Abraham Lincoln. There was nothing Horatio Algerish about his career. Like Washington and Jefferson he was a product of wealth and aristocracy.

He was born on January 30, 1882, the second son of James Roosevelt, a descendent on his paternal side of early Dutch settlers in the Hudson River valley. His mother was the second wife of his father. Franklin was her only child. She was Sara Delano, who lived until her son had spent eight years in the White House, left him a fortune that had been made in the shipping trade. Earlier Roosevelts had been members of the Dutch Reformed Church. Franklin's mother brought him up as an Episcopalian. He eventually became a senior lay officer in the parish church.

The Delano or maternal side of Mr. Roosevelt's ancestry was traced through a long line of Flanders knights back to 1096, by Daniel Webster Delano, a fourth cousin of the President.

"Earliest authentic records show the family stemming from Hugues De Lannoy, who was count of the tiny French village of Lannoy in 1096," Mr. Delano said.

Mr. Roosevelt himself once said he had never had enough interest or leisure to trace his own ancestral records back farther than the 300 years the family had lived on this continent.

First of the family to reach America was Phillippe De Lannoy, who sailed from Holland as a 16-year-old cabin boy in 1621 on the vessel Fortune. He settled at Duxbury, Mass., where his house was built between the homes of Miles Standish and John Alden.

Phillippe De Lannoy's grandchildren, who were sea captains sailing clipper ships in the China tea trade, changed the family name to Delano. There was an Amasa Delano who became a ship captain in his twenties and sailed to all parts of the world.

F.D.R. was not the first President to be a Delano; President Grant's mother was a Delano.

There were maritime forbears on both sides of his family. In the paternal line was Nicholas J. Roosevelt, who was associated with Robert Fulton in the introduction of the steamboat. The apparatus whereby the ship was propelled by vertical wheels, was Nicholas Roosevelt's patent and this was credited with making Fulton's Clermont a success.

Genealogical enthusiasts traced a relationship between F.R.D. and Winston Churchill, through John Cooke, a Mayflower passenger. They also found a similarly distant relationship between F.D.R. and King George VI of Britain.

Franklin's father, James, was himself moderately wealthy at the time the future President was born. He was then 54 years old. He had been president of the Louisville & New Albany Railroad and was Vice President of the Delaware & Hudson R.R. He never had much taste for business and he retired to the life of a country gentlemen at Hyde Park while Franklin was in his infancy. He died in 1900, when the future President was 18 years old. One of the canards uttered against F.D.R. in a Presidential campaign was that his father had drawn his will so as to keep his estate out of the hands of his son, "because he knew he couldn't handle money." This is refuted by the will, still on file in the Surrogate's

THE PRESIDENT'S MOTHER, NEE SARA DELANO, WAS THE SECOND WIFE OF HIS FATHER. FDR WAS HER ONLY CHILD.

Court in Dutchess County. It devises a major share of the estate to Franklin.

Franklin got his early education at home from his father (who among other things founded his knowledge and interest in geography through a stamp collection) and from tutors, and when 14 entered the exclusive Groton school to prepare for Harvard. He was then already well-traveled and he knew French, Spanish and German. He had won a reputation as an ornithologist through his observation of bird life in his home Dutchess county. He had no difficulties at Groton and at Harvard he passed automatically into the select clubs, including the Hasty Pudding. He was chosen for Alpha Delta Phi. By the time he was graduated, an A.B., he had won the coveted Phi Beta Kappa key. He had also officiated as editor of *The Crimson*.

At Harvard Franklin Roosevelt first gave signs of having ideas radically different from those of most persons in his social strata. He became identified with progressive movements on the campus and was the leader of some of them. Significantly, he majored at Harvard in economics and international law.

Young Franklin was handsome and rated as considerable of a matrimonial "catch." He married a childhood sweetheart on St. Patrick's Day, in 1905, when he had been graduated from Harvard and was going on to Columbia University to study his chosen profession, law. His bride was a distant cousin, Eleanor Roosevelt. She was a favorite niece of the then President Theodore Roosevelt, and the President gave the bride away. Franklin was also a relative of "T.R.", but more distantly; and "T.R.'s" brother, Elliott, had been Franklin's godfather.

The young couple settled down in a house built for them by Franklin's mother in Manhattan, and he began practice of law there in 1907. Family connections and the ability he showed on his early cases brought him a good practice quickly. Almost immediately he entered politics. Roosevelts on the "T.R." side of the family were Republicans, but Franklin's father had been a Democrat, and that became Franklin's party. In 1910, he contested for a State senatorial seat in a district that had long been rock-ribbed Republican. He upset the political dope and won, and immediately upon entering the legislature at Albany became conspicuous for his talents as a political tactician who did not truckle to machine bosses. He confirmed forebodings of "Big Tim" Sullivan, chief lieutenant of Tammany Leader

Charles Murphy. Election night, as Sullivan's eye ran down the list of successful Democrats and noted Franklin's, he said: "If we've caught a Roosevelt we'd better take him down and drop him off the dock. The kid is likely to do for us what the Colonel is doing for the Republican party—split it wide open."

One of the stories F.D.R. liked to tell was about his first triumph in behind-the-scenes politics. He was still in his twenties, serving his first term in the New York State Senate, when utilities lobbyists tried to get the legislature to elect William Sheehan as U. S. Senator. In those days Senators were still elected by legislatures.

Roosevelt was a leader of progressive Democrats and Republicans who fought the choice of Sheehan. In the midst of the battle, a Democratic senator from Seneca County named Charlie Cusack, who was 73 years old then, told Roosevelt the mortgage on the Cusack farm would be foreclosed if he, Cusack, voted against Sheehan. Inasmuch as the Roosevelt forces then had a majority of only three votes, this was a serious matter.

F.D.R. investigated and found it was true the utilities interests had pressured the bank. He raised the money to pay off the mortgage. Two others were similarly threatened with foreclosures, and refinancing had to be arranged for them.

"Then in the Ten Eyck Hotel, Cusack sat with other legislators, drinking beer," F.D.R. related. "At midnight the bar closed and one suggested they go to a blind-tiger. They were there drinking when the place was pinched."

The legislators feared reactions in their districts if their arrests were recorded. "We're legislators—you can't arrest us," they argued.

"The hell we can't," said the policemen. One legislator said he knew Charlie Murphy, head of Tammany, who could exert influence on Pinkie McCabe, political boss in Albany. He slipped out to phone Murphy, and came back to report:

"It's ok, boys. I talked to Charlie and he talked to McCabe. Pinkie says it's fixed. But there's one thing we've got to do in return." He looked at Cusack. "You've got to vote for Sheehan."

"Well," drawled Cusack, "I've been thinkin' this over. I'm 73. In Seneca they call me 'Uncle Charlie.' But I figure if they read I'm arrested in this kind of a house they'll send me back to Albany the rest of my life. Bring on the police!"

The raid had been framed by utilities lobby

agents who'd shadowed Cusack and his party. That was the end of the incident.

Tammany surrendered its effort to elect Sheehan on the 60th ballot and accepted James A. O'Gorman, who had been chosen as a compromise candidate in a caucus of insurgents at Roosevelt's house.

At twenty-nine, the young politician had won his spurs as an aggressive liberal who worked out definite programs and then sought to carry them out with a dogged determination.

Mrs. Roosevelt from the beginning was an active political partner of her ambitious husband. The Roosevelt home in Albany was a constant meeting place for the young insurgents whom the new senator had gathered about him, and Mrs. Roosevelt played an important part in aligning them on a common front with F.D.R.

In 1912, she and F.D.R. acquired an important helper in this. He was Louis McHenry Howe, an Albany newspaper correspondent who was a natural-born politician. Roosevelt as a young state senator aroused in Howe an interest that turned into a strong admiration and then into a determination to elect him President of the United States.

The 1912 session of the Legislature was not a happy one for Roosevelt. The old line politicians in his party were gunning for him now. As his term in the senate expired he was faced with the task of winning without any of the machine's support. At the end of September, 1912, at the time of the conventions, he became ill of typhoid fever and was not able to raise a voice in his campaign.

Howe took charge. He used full-page advertisements in the newspapers—a thing unheard of in those days—and on the night of election day, although he had hitherto been barred from the sick room, he was permitted to telephone to Roosevelt that the election was won.

At just about the same time Mr. Roosevelt was making a name for himself in Albany, another Democrat down in New Jersey was pursuing the same liberal course. This man was Woodrow Wilson, and he and Roosevelt became fast friends. When the 1912 convention came Roosevelt went to Baltimore a Wilson man and aided in turning the tide from Champ Clark to Wilson.

Wilson's election brought young Roosevelt into the national political picture. For the new President remembered the young Democrat who had pressed so influentially for his nomination

with the key New York delegation. When his Secretary of the Navy, Josephus Daniels, sought an Assistant Secretary, the name of Franklin Roosevelt was presented. It was a post the earlier President Roosevelt had once held.

Franklin Roosevelt's service in the Navy Department might have been brief and his whole subsequent career changed had the outcome of an election in 1914 been different. He was the candidate of the anti-Tammany wing of the party for United States Senator in the New York Democratic primary that year. He was defeated by the Tammany candidate, James W. Gerard, subsequently Wilson's ambassador to Germany, and he remained as Assistant Secretary of the Navy through the war years, in charge of civilian personnel, Navy yards and docks, purchasing and supplies. During this time dozens of reforms in the department were attributed to the already well-developed Roosevelt bent for innovation and disregarding precedent. He was in charge of inspection of U. S. naval forces in European waters from July to September, 1918, and in charge of demobilization of our naval establishment overseas after the war, and these experiences gave him valuable background for dealing with problems that were to confront him in the White House 20 years later.

His absence in Washington did not remove him from the New York political picture. Howe, Mrs. Roosevelt and the liberals in the Democratic party in the state made sure that it didn't. In 1918, he was proposed for the governorship. F.D.R. declined. Just before going overseas, he wrote President Wilson:

"I entirely forgot on Sunday evening to speak to you of a personal matter which might come up during my absence—the question of my nomination for the Governorship of New York. I have tried in every way to stop it, but some of your friends and mine have talked of the possibility of forcing this while I am away, and of asking you to encourage me to accept it.

"I sincerely hope the matter will not come up. I have made my position entirely clear that my duty lies in my present work—not only my duty to you and the country, but my duty to myself. If I were at any time to leave the Assistant Secretaryship it could only be for active service.

"Furthermore, may I say that I am very certain that it would be a grave mistake for either you or any member of the Administration to ask that I give up war work for what is frankly very much of a political job in these times. I cannot accept such a nomination at this time with honesty or honor to myself. I think I have put off all danger of it, but in case you are appealed to, I want you to know what I feel—and I know too that you will understand and that you will not listen to the appeal."

Opportunity again presented in 1920 for him to become candidate for governor in New York State. He rejected it again and sponsored the nomination of Alfred E. Smith. At the Democratic national convention that year, F.D.R. placed the name of Smith in nomination for the Presidency. The party passed over Smith for James M. Cox, but named F.D.R. as Cox's running mate.

The campaign cast Roosevelt for the first time in the role of advocate of a world league for maintenance of peace by force against conservative isolationists, and F.D.R. waged a vigorous campaign for vindication of Wilson's commitments to Britain and the other Allied powers.

When the campaign was over, with Harding and Coolidge elected, Mr. Roosevelt moved his family back to New York. It was a large family now: he and Mrs. Roosevelt had five children, Anna, James, Elliott, Franklin D., Jr. and John. He resumed the practise of law and settled down to what was for him a quiet life.

His life was to be changed completely within a year. For in August 1921, while the family was at the Roosevelt family summer home at Campobello, New Brunswick, he was stricken with poliomyelitis. It left him paralyzed from the waist down.

His long battle to get back on his feet not only resulted in epochal chapters in American political and economic history, but it contributed new knowledge to the treatment of the disease that had crippled him.

In a talk at a Thanksgiving Day party for fellow patients at Warm Springs, Ga., the year after he became President, Mr. Roosevelt gave details of his battle for recovery from the paralysing effects of infantile paralysis: and the establishment of the Warm Springs Foundation:

"In 1924, I was taking treatments from Dr. Lovett in Boston who, at that time, was believed to have done more in the after-treatment of infantile paralysis than almost anybody. I got talking with Dr. Lovett about experimental work with polio and he said, 'You know, I found an interesting thing last summer. Most of my patients come from New England, and a great many of them come from seashores. I told all of them to swim as much as they possibly could and it is an interesting fact that the patients who went down to Buzzards Bay and Long Island Sound, where the waters were warm and where they could spend a great many minutes of the day in the water swimming around, seemed to improve in their muscles a great deal more than those of my patients who went to the North Shore or to the coast of Maine where the water is cold and you can only stay in for three or four or five minutes. Therefore, I have started a little shallow tank in the Children's Hospital of Boston to see if we cannot learn something from exercising muscles in the medium of water instead of just exercising them on tables.'

"I did not give very much attention to this then, although I thought he was pursuing an interesting course in developing this theory.

"About September first I got a letter from Mr. Peabody and Mr. Peabody said, 'Here is an interesting letter that I am enclosing from Mr. Tom Loyless, who is running Warm Springs for me.'

"Mr. Loyless told about a young man by the name of Josephs from Columbus [Ga.] who had come to Warm Springs after an attack of infantile paralysis. He could not walk at all. There was just a public pool here then, but he had taught himself to use his legs in the water, to get his feet down to the bottom and to walk around on the bottom. Later on he found he could walk in shallower water all the time, and he kept on doing that until he found that he could walk on dry land.

"Well, I put two and two together and I said to myself, 'This confirms Dr. Lovett's theory.' Meanwhile, Dr. Lovett had gone on a trip to Europe and unfortunately had died over there, so I was unable to consult him.

"But I spoke to Peabody and it was arranged for me to go to Hart's Cottage, now Mr. Pierson's cottage. We came down in the autumn. The only people who were here when we arrived were Mr. and Mrs. Loyless and old Mr. Watts, a postman, and it is perfectly true that he read everybody's postcards. In fact, he read so many postcards that it took him almost all day to make the delivery of the mail to the Loyless cottage and mine.

"When we came down, there was no doctor around here; there was nobody in charge, or anything of a medical nature. I went down to what is now the public pool. It was rather simple in those days.

"I stayed here for a month and I improved so

much that I came back the following spring. But people had heard about it.

"One day Mr. Loyless and some of the neighbors—the Harts, Miss Wilkins and Josephs and some of us—were sitting around when a messenger came up the hill to Mr. Loyless and said, 'Two people have been carried off the train down at the station. What shall we do with them. Neither of them can walk.'

"Well, we held a consultation. It was long before anything was done here in the way of a hotel or cottages. We decided that we could take care of them in the village overnight, and then, in a couple of days we could fix up what is now *The Wreck* and put them in it. Well, before we could put that cottage in order, eight others had arrived.

"We did not know what to do with them so I sent for Dr. Johnson. He came and looked them over and guaranteed that they did not have heart trouble or something from which they would suddenly die, and he recommended cream and fattening diets for some and he recommended very little food for some of the others.

"And then I undertook to be doctor and physiotherapist, all rolled into one. I taught Fred Botts to swim. I taught them all to at least play around in the water.

"I called that my medical practice, the first and last time that I have ever practiced medicine and physio-therapy. After I get through at the White House, I hope the medical fraternity will allow me to come back and practice here. I feel I would be rather good at giving exercises in the water. At least I have had more exercise in the water, over a longer period of time, than anybody else in captivity in this country.

"And then, we came down the following year, 1926, which, in a way, was the most interesting period we have ever had here because for the first time we had adequate medical supervision. We were a very small group of patients; I think there were twenty-five. Dr. Hubbard and Miss Mahoney were in charge and every step we took was an experiment. In order to make both ends meet, we tried to run the Inn as a hotel at the same time that we were taking care of these 25 patients.

"Mr. Pope and I were the Foundation that year. Mr. Pope and I had long conferences. We started with a band of five pieces; but I think we spent an hour talking over the question of whether we could afford a band of five pieces or whether we should reduce it to three pieces. However, we managed to get by, and the following spring of 1927 the Foundation itself was truly launched."

From that ordeal with infantile paralysis, F.D.R. emerged with the confidence that he could master any catastrophe. Even his doctors told him, "There are few men with the strength to make that fight."

A Roosevelt intimate, Morris Ernst, the New York lawyer, in an appraisal of F.D.R. and Mrs. Roosevelt written several months before the President's death, said the elements in his makeup that really distinguished Franklin D. Roosevelt stemmed from his infirmity, because out of a calamity he had accepted life as it came. Compassion and understanding took the place of hate. There was a peculiar sort of joyousness in him, and humorless people were confused by him because much of his approach to other people was through jests and needling with the hope of a mental joust.

Mr. Ernst observed Mrs. Roosevelt to have been essential to F.D.R., and for one reason for which most other people failed to come near him —that she stood up to him; and people around him got on with him because they were his echoes, she got on because she was tough with him.

During his rebuilding of his health, Mrs. Roosevelt and Louis Howe saw to it that his political fortunes did not decline. His illness did not affect his political acumen and with their aid, he kept his formidable position in New York politics. He led the fight to have the progressive Alfred E. Smith made the Democratic standard-bearer in 1924 against Coolidge, but when the conservative John W. Davis was nominated instead, Roosevelt, the liberal, did not lessen his efforts in behalf of the party ticket. He knew there must be unity if the Democrats were to be restored to power. Davis began his campaign with a speech at Roosevelt's Hyde Park estate.

Oddly enough, in 1920, Roosevelt gave some thought to the possibility of Herbert Hoover becoming a Democratic candidate for President. He and Hoover had become friends during the war, when Hoover had made a record as food administrator in this country and relief dispenser abroad. Hoover was then a "man without a party," and F.D.R. sought to bring him within the Democratic lines. Before he succeeded, others had induced Hoover to declare himself as a Republican; he went into Harding's cabinet as Secretary of Commerce. Smith became Roosevelt's choice for President. After having nominated him in the national conventions in 1920 and 1924, F.D.R.'s efforts were finally rewarded in 1928, when Smith became the party candidate against Hoover. It was decided that Roosevelt himself would be the best man to carry New York State and to hold the social gains which had been made in Smith's terms in the gubernatorial chair.

Smith lost New York State and the nation in the Presidential balloting but Roosevelt won the governorship by 25,000. So well did he satisfy the people that two years later he was re-elected by a majority of nearly a million. In those days, you could find the Governor of New York almost anywhere except in the Governor's office. Perhaps up along the Erie Canal, finding out why more shippers didn't use it. Or driving down a dusty country road to see first-hand why some farms don't pay.

Mr. Roosevelt in his work as Governor of New York had to lick the same bugaboo that later developed in his Presidential campaign—that of his enemies who portrayed him as a man too physically weak to fulfill all the requirements of the office. This he effectively disproved by his record of work as Governor, but when he entered the Presidential race, he had to beat it again.

Charles Michelson, who was the Democratic National Committee's publicity chief, has told what happened when he and James A. Farley, the party chairman, called a conference in Washington to discuss the advisability of Mr. Roosevelt conducting a "front porch" campaign. "It was decided that such a swing around the circle involved too many dangers," he wrote in *The Ghost Talks*. "The candidate's physical condition was being emphasized by Republican propagandists, and there was the danger that he might collapse in mid-career, or, in the course of a hundred impromptu train-end speeches, he might well make a slip that would be disastrous.

"So Farley and I repaired to the governor's mansion at Albany and reported that the high board of strategy agreed with us, and with Howe, that the project was too dangerous.

"The Governor listened to our report and announced:

" 'Well, I'm going anyhow.'

" 'Why take a chance?' was the query shot at him.

" 'Because I want to,' was his reply. 'And,' he added. 'I'm not going to take a doctor along either.'

"So he went on the pilgrimage. He knew his capacity for endurance better than we did; he knew that the best answer to his foe's insinuations of feeble health was to show himself to the people and demonstrate that he had the fortitude and the stamina to take what a term in the Presidency involved."

The dramatic flight of Mr. Roosevelt from Albany to Chicago to shatter precedent and immediately accept the nomination in 1932 did a lot to dispel doubts of those who were preaching the doctrine that Mr. Roosevelt was a "parlor pink", a man of indecision. Bluntly and straightforwardly, the new nominee stated his opinions and told the thousands in the convention hall that he would leave no room for doubt as to his feelings on any subject. He proved this in the campaign he conducted, and the nation elected him to the Presidency over the Republican nominee and then President, Hoover, by a majority that had never before been approached.

The new President made changes swiftly. Breaking precedent again on inauguration day by leaving the reviewing stand while the parade was still on, he swore in his cabinet and went into action to meet the banking crisis that had been developing through the nation. In lightning fashion, he called Congress into special session, declared a nation-wide bank holiday that closed every financial institution temporarily, and obtained from Congress powers to meet the emergency commensurate with those conferred upon a wartime President.

Working with his first Secretary of the Treasury, William H. Woodin, Mr. Roosevelt mapped out and put into effect a complete new financial set-up for the United States. A guarantee of bank deposits up to $5,000 was one feature.

In the first 105 days he occupied the White House, Mr. Roosevelt whipped through Congress the following:

The Emergency Banking Act;

The Economy Act, later repealed;

The Agricultural Adjustment Act, later invalidated by the Supreme Court;

The National Industrial Recovery Act, later tossed out by the Court;

The Tennessee Valley Authority Act;

The Civilian Conservation Corps Act—of which Mr. Roosevelt was especially proud;

The Home Owners' Loan Act;

The Railroad Co-ordinator Act;

The Glass-Steagal Bank Act;

The 3.2 Beer Act;

The $500,000,000 Emergency Relief Act, forerunner of many months of heavy spending to make good the pledge that "no one shall starve";

The Securities Act;

The Wagner Employment Exchange Act;

The Gold Clause Resolution, under which Mr. Roosevelt devalued the American dollar and returned it to parity with the British pound, and

Amendments expanding the power of the Reconstruction Finance Corporation.

Mr. Roosevelt, the scion of aristocracy and wealth, constantly fought the battle of the underdog—of "the ill-clad, ill-nourished, ill-housed."

He sponsored the Wagner National Labor Relations Act, which guaranteed the workman the right to organize without company interference. He set up the Rural Electrification Administration and the Resettlement Administration, as well as the Federal Communications and the United States Maritime Commissions.

Prohibition repeal was perhaps the most outstanding example of Mr. Roosevelt's ability to get action quickly through previously slow-moving governmental machinery. The nation had been dragging along, complaining against the dry law for years, with both political parties straddling or running away from the issue. Finally, in 1932, the Democratic Party took a fairly firm stand for prohibition repeal at its Chicago Convention.

Mr. Roosevelt kept the pledge. Promptly after entering the White House, he persuaded Congress to restore 3.2 beer and within a year the States had repealed the 18th Amendment. Thousands of unemployed were put back to work by the distilling, brewing and allied industries, and organized crime was deprived of a fabulous source of treasure.

Presidential mail jumped to enormous proportions, with citizens writing about their smallest wants to the man in the White House. More than 18 months after his election, Mr. Roosevelt's mail was more than 4,000 items daily. On his birthday a nation united as one man to gladly carry out the wish of the President, expressed in an unguarded moment some months before, that he would like to see a million dollar endowment of the Warm Springs, Ga., infantile paralysis foundation. Every year on the President's birthday some 25,000 "birthday parties" were held throughout the nation, all proceeds going to the gradually enlargening health resort.

He used the radio more regularly and with more effect than any other head of state any-

where. No other person ever spoke to so many humans at a time. With an acute awareness of the potentialities of broadcasting that characterized all his use of the media of public relations, he studied and rehearsed until he had no peer among radio speakers in the world.

The Roosevelt battle with the utilities interests was one of the most spectacular features of his White House career. Early in the New Deal, Mr. Roosevelt set up TVA as a big federal power experiment in the Tennessee Valley. This was followed by construction of Bonneville, Grand Coulee and Fort Peck Dams. Private interests feared a nation-wide federal power system with these generating units and Boulder Dam as a nucleus.

Appealing to the sympathies of the ultimate consumer, Mr. Roosevelt called for a government "yardstick" that would help force the price of electric current down. He demanded that the utilities evaluate themselves properly and wring the water out of their capitalization. He forced through legislation applying the "death sentence" to holding companies.

In this fight Mr. Roosevelt coined the expression "Economic Royalists," which will probably go down in history along with his "New Deal" and "Forgotten Man."

Another act that won Mr. Roosevelt the enmity of a large element of financial interests was creation of the Securities and Exchange Commission to rule the stock market with an iron hand. By putting all of big business on the defensive, he gave force and effect to demands that had long been made within industries for reforms.

His social reforms had now reached tremendous proportions. They culminated in a Social Security Act for the entire nation.

Perhaps the most important message ever sent by F.D.R. or any other President to the Congress concerning domestic policy, was that on January 17, 1935, reported in the following International News Service dispatch by Kenneth Clark:

"Washington, Jan. 17—Asserting that the country cannot be guaranteed against future depressions, but that their effects can be mitigated, President Roosevelt today asked Congress to enact a broad-gauged program of social security legislation designed to help what he has described as the 'under-privileged' in the American economic system.

"His program embraced:

"1. Unemployment compensation, with the Federal Government holding the purse strings and the individual States administering the plan, to be financed by a pay-roll tax of 3 per cent, jointly contributed by the employer and employe alone, as the States decide.

"2. Old age pensions, with the Federal Government matching the States dollar-for-dollar, the age minimum being 65.

"3. Federal aid to the States in caring for dependent and crippled children.

"4. Federal aid to state and local public health agencies, with a strengthening of the U. S. Public Health Service.

"Mr. Roosevelt estimated the cost to the Federal Government of this four-point program at approximately $100,000,000 the first year.

"At the President's behest, Congressional leaders gave precedence over all other legislation to the social security program, which was boiled down into a single bill introduced jointly by Senator Wagner, of New York, and Representative Lewis, of Maryland. The legislature contemplated that the cost may subsequently rise to $200,000,000 a year. Public hearings on the bill will be begun Tuesday by the Senate Finance Committee.

"The President accompanied his message to Congress with a voluminous 35,000-word explanatory report on the program, prepared by his Committee on Economic Security. The Wagner legislation was modeled closely upon the recommendations of this committee, whose chairman was Secretary of Labor Frances Perkins.

" 'No one can guarantee this country against the dangers of future depressions,' he said, 'but we can reduce these dangers.

" 'We can eliminate many of the factors that cause economic depressions and we can provide the means of mitigating their results. This plan for economic security is at once a measure of prevention and a method of alleviation.

" 'We pay now for the dreadful consequence of economic insecurity—and dearly. This plan presents a more equitable and infinitely less expensive means of meeting those costs. We cannot afford to neglect the plain duty before us.'

"Mr. Roosevelt did not go into details in his message, but the accompanying report and legislation did."

He had forecast the measure in a message to Congress on January 4th in which he had said:

"Continued dependence upon relief induces a spiritual and moral disintegration fundamentally destructive to the national fibre. To dole out relief in this way is to administer a narcotic, a subtle destroyer of the human spirit."

He had already brought temporary aid and employment to millions through nation-wide Public Works Administration and Civilian Conservation plans that were the subject of bitter controversy.

In affecting all his reforms, F.D.R. naturally had opposition and all his genius and finesse as a politician were required to accomplish some of them. But he was not afraid to buck the weight and influence of organized groups. He had shown that in vetoing the Soldier Bonus Bill passed by Congress in 1935. He said:

"I hold that able-bodied veterans should be accorded no different treatment than that accorded citizens who wore no uniforms during the war, but also served to win it. . . . Veterans suffering from depression can best be aided by rehabilitation of the whole country. A veteran's interests following discharge became identical with those of his country."

It was with the Supreme Court that he most often came to grips in the earlier days of his Administration. Throughout 1935 the high tribunal delivered a number of reverses to his New Deal emergency program—notably NRA and AAA.

When the Supreme Court, on May 27, 1935, unanimously held the National Industrial Relations Act illegal, Mr. Roosevelt fought back.

Four days later, at an historic press conference, the President told reporters the Court had taken the nation "back to the horse and buggy days" by invalidating the Administration's efforts to regulate hours and wages. He promised a solution would be found.

"If the Constitution makes the Federal program for regulating economic conditions impossible, it may be necessary to amend the Constitution," he declared.

Playing canny politics, Mr. Roosevelt did not make the Supreme Court an issue in his 1936 campaign for re-election. His opponent was the Republican Governor Alf M. Landon, of Kansas. F.D.R. toured the country in an electrifying campaign that became bitter, with Republicans focusing their attack on the WPA. They attacked the entire program as "boondoggling," a tag pinned on the agency's work by Western ranch hands employed under it during idle winter months. The Republicans further sought to discredit the WPA by accusing the administrative heads of herding their project workers into the Roosevelt camp under threat of dismissal.

Alfred E. Smith had attacked the New Deal in a speech early in the year in which he threatened to "take a walk" from the party, and had joined Bainbridge Colby, James A. Reed, Joseph B. Ely and Daniel F. Cohalan in an appeal to the Democratic convention to repudiate the New Deal and nominate "a genuine Democrat."

At the same time Mr. Roosevelt's strength grew among the masses, especially of organized labor. Union leaders organized labor leagues to produce millions of votes for the President.

The nation went to the polls on Nov. 3 after more than $13,000,000 had been spent by the parties in the campaign. When the results were in President Roosevelt and Vice President John Nance Garner had been re-elected in the greatest sweep in the nation's history, carrying every State in the union except Maine and Vermont.

Taking anew the oath of office in a driving rain on January 20, 1937, he declared: "The autocratic powers have been challenged and beaten. The legend that they were invincible . . . has been shattered."

He returned to his attack on the Supreme Court, and suffered his first major political reverse.

He boldly proposed to Congress in 1937 that all federal justices over the age of 70 either retire or have a younger man appointed to help them. At that time, this would have given Mr. Roosevelt six potential appointments to the Supreme Court.

A well organized wave of opposition set in to defeat this proposal but the President was adamant. The Senate was locked in its most gruelling debate since the League of Nations fight.

It is a matter of record that in early April of 1937 Mr. Roosevelt could have accepted a compromise of two appointees to the top bench and won his fight. He and the late Joseph T. Robinson, of Arkansas, then Majority Leader of the Senate, decided to fight on for six. They lost the vote in Congress, but in another respect F.D.R. won. The Supreme Court's decisions became less conservative. Eventually, F.D.R. appointed most of its members.

Undaunted, Mr. Roosevelt swung to the west coast in the late summer of 1937, arranging his train schedule to pass through the bailiwicks of such western Senate opponents to his court plan as Burton K. Wheeler, of Montana, Joseph O'Mahoney, of Wyoming, and Edward R. Burke, of Nebraska.

Everywhere, he received tremendous crowds.

Literally millions cheered him back and forth across the continent. In his speeches, Mr. Roosevelt pledged himself anew to restore the hour and wage provisions of NRA and the surplus crop control provision of AAA.

In the course of that trip, Mr. Roosevelt listened carefully for a backfire to his appointment of Hugo L. Black, former Democratic Senator from Alabama, to the Supreme Court succeeding Justice Van Devanter. He found only an apathetic interest in the west to disclosures that Black had once been a member of the Ku Klux Klan, and returned to Washington to issue a call for a special session of Congress, proposing hour-wage and farm legislation as promised.

Meanwhile, business had become stagnant again. In the fall of 1937, the stock market broke in a manner somewhat reminiscent of the famous "Black Friday" of 1929.

Mr. Roosevelt swung into action with characteristic vigor to meet this new threat to the economic equilibrium. He announced that the 1938-39 budget would be put in balance with a sharp curbing of relief expenditures. He agreed to a revision of burdensome taxes. He undertook to make peace with the large utilities groups by promising they need fear no expansion of federal competition—at the same time suggesting they expand themselves and thus help the sagging heavy industries. He mapped out a new housing program designed to attract private capital through government cooperation.

For more than two years, the Chief Executive steadfastly avoided answering questions on his decision whether to cast aside precedent once again and seek a third four-year-term in the White House. To Washington correspondents, the question became futility itself, and they refrained from asking it for fear of bringing the Presidential anger down about their heads.

Yet at the 1940 Democratic convention in Chicago, the President permitted himself to be "drafted" for a third term, and, with the presence of Harry Hopkins, who had succeeded a host of other "Brain Trusters" as a Roosevelt confidant, in Chicago, there were charges, never completely answered, that he had "engineered" his own draft in behind-the-scenes maneuvers.

His acceptance brought into the open a split between himself and his longtime political comrade, Postmaster-General James Farley. Farley, devoted to the political party that he had played so instrumental a part in developing, continued as a faithful worker until after the elections that fall. But immediately afterwards, he resigned all his federal and party positions, with the exception of his New York State position in the Democratic Party, and, thereafter worked against F.D.R.'s efforts to control the party.

The White House, echoing Mr. Roosevelt's sentiments, often blamed Farley when the Chief Executive suffered political setbacks by his own party. The differences between Mr. Roosevelt and Farley, stemming from the third term controversy, left a mark on the Democratic Party which remained through the balance of the Chief Executive's time, and even the urgencies of war and political unity could not heal the schism.

President Roosevelt's opponent in the 1940 race was Wendell L. Willkie, a "traditional" Democrat, who himself had bolted the party and won over the Republican convention by the force of his personality and statements.

Both contestants were eye-to-eye on foreign policy, and on many domestic issues as well, the only differences being on methods to be employed to gain goals.

President Roosevelt was swept into office by a comfortable majority, but, in defeat, Wendell Willkie polled a heavy vote, and continued to be a political force to be reckoned with until his death.

The President subsequently okehed a trip by Willkie around the world as an unofficial American spokesman, and in a "fireside talk" he said:

"The dictators cannot seem to realize that here in America our people can maintain two parties and at the same time maintain an inviolate and indivisible nation. The totalitarian mentality is too narrow to comprehend the greatness of a people who can be divided in party allegiance at election time, but remain united in devotion to their country and to the ideals of democracy at all times.

"In our country, disagreements among us are expressed in the polling place. In the dictatorships, disagreements are suppressed in the concentration camp."

B Y 1941, when he began his 3rd term, foreign affairs had taken precedence in Roosevelt attentions to domestic plans and policies and he embarked on an era of personal and confidential era of statesmanship in American history.

He left his indelible mark on a whole world thrown abruptly into a life-and-death struggle between the forces of democracy and totali-

tarianism. Here too, his decisions were firm and his actions swift, and his the dominant voice.

The Chief Executive was an avowed internationalist during, and in the years immediately preceding the outbreak of war, and his hopes and plans for a better post-war era for the United States had as their cornerstone a world governed for the mutual benefit of all nations.

President Roosevelt foresaw the inevitability of American participation in the war as a belligerent long before many in his own administration. He called for preparedness expenditures on at least one occasion when Congress was unwilling to comply, and led all others in his demands for war materials and war-productive industries.

Through Lend-Lease laws, the productive might of industrial and agricural America transformed into the "arsenal of democracy"— was thrown behind Great Britain and Russia, before the United States formally entered the fight.

The Lend-Lease expenditures for new war production plants gave the United States the industrial skeleton on which it was to build the largest "arsenal" the world had ever known.

And, in contrast to the first World War when the United States armies were largely supplied and equipped by her Allies, by 1943, after a year of war, America was the greatest producer of war planes, tanks, guns, and ammunition, of any nation on either side of the fight.

After a dramatic conference on the high seas with Britain's premier, Winston Churchill, President Roosevelt set the goal of the American people in the war in the "four freedoms"—freedom of speech, freedom of worship, freedom from want, freedom from fear for the world.

Though he foresaw the inevitability of the conflict, in the months immediately preceding the Japanese attack on Pearl Harbor that brought formal declarations of war, President Roosevelt sought repeatedly to avert the conflict.

The United States diplomatic talks with Japan, published in a "White Paper," reveal in detail the actions in bad-faith of the Japanese war lords, and document the American efforts to continue conversations in the face of our leaders' knowledge of this double dealing and deceit.

In his dealing with Hitler and Mussolini, the Chief Executive displayed the same patience he had in his diplomatic efforts with Japan. But wisely, while talking softly, he whittled a big stick.

HIS HAPPIEST DAYS WERE SPENT AMID RUSTIC BEAUTY OF HYDE PARK, WHICH HE GAVE AS A GIFT TO THE NATION.

HE BUILT THIS LIBRARY TO PRESERVE ALL HIS PAPERS.

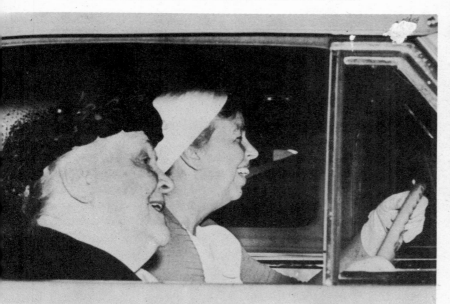

A LAST PHOTO OF HIS MOTHER. MRS. F.D.R. IS WITH HER.

THE ANCESTRAL HOME and a fortune of over a million were willed to him when his mother died in 1941. He was always more at ease there than in the White House surroundings, preferring an informal life.

His failure with Hitler, Mussolini and Hirohito was no measure of his calibre as diplomat and statesman. That was shown better and more conclusively by how he prepared the way for the final overwhelming defeat of Germany, Japan and Italy by bringing together the Allied leaders with himself, first at Casablanca, and then at Cairo and Teheran, to mold the United States, Great Britain, Russia, and China into one great instrument of warring vengeance to crush the Axis.

Mr. Churchill has established the fact that when the grand strategy of the Anglo-American blow against Germany and Italy was being formulated by the combined chiefs of staffs in Washington in the early days of the war, it was Mr. Roosevelt who suggested and insisted that the first move be the liberation of French North Africa, where a great Allied base could be established for further blows against Hitlerite Europe itself.

One observer suggested that President Roosevelt's method of operating was to contribute all he could to discussions with his Chiefs of Staff leading up to military decisions, then to indicate in a broad sense what course he thought it wise to explore, but, after that, to leave the details to the military and naval leaders whose responsibility it was to execute them.

The record of the years 1942, 1943, 1944 and 1945 is an epic of American leadership in world affairs—a leadership established by F.D.R.

In January of 1943, came his flight over the South Atlantic to meet Prime Minister Churchill at Casablanca where the two, with their staffs, planned the smashing debacle for Field Marshal Rommel's famed Afrika Korps that followed in April and May in Tunisia; the devastating succeeding attack against Sicily; and the invasion of Italy late in the summer that brought Italy's capitulation and gave the Allies complete control of the vital Mediterranean lifeline.

It was Roosevelt who, at Casablanca, recoined the phrase and enunciated the determination that became the Allied battle cry of victory— "Unconditional Surrender!"

Then, the following August, the two statesmen again met in Quebec, Canada. Here they mapped Pacific strategy that saw the successive fall of Attu and Kiska, wresting the Aleutian foothold from the Japanese, and smashing their critical threat of an invasion of the North American continent. Here, too, was laid the plan for the reduction of Tarawa and full occupation of the Mar-

shalls, and the succeeding thrust into the midst of Japan's long-held island empire at Saipan in the Marianas.

Then, in the following November, the President sprang his greatest surprise of the year. Secretary of State Cordell Hull earlier went to Moscow and there began the cementing of American-Soviet relations and combined war plans. Roosevelt crossed the Atlantic again, flew to Cairo, met Churchill and Chiang Kai-shek, mapped plans for the Allied thrusts in Assam and China in an effort to retake the Burma Road.

Then he flew on to Teheran where he and Churchill sat down with Marshal Stalin and synchronized the plans for invasion of German-held Europe across the channel from England with Russian blows on Germany from the East. They made no secret of their intentions. They warned Hitler that he could expect to be smote from the south, from the east and from the west until Germany's military power was forever broken.

This promise and warning brought fruit on June 6, 1944, when Anglo-American troops, borne from southern England to the Normandy peninsula by an armada of 4,000 ships, breached the Germans' vaunted Atlantic wall in the greatest invasion in history. Its immediate success was the beginning of the end for Hitler.

Mr. Roosevelt had now turned his attention almost wholly on the war, but not for an instant did he recede from his long fight for the common man. He found time to push plans for taking care of the war veterans when peace returned, of finding jobs for them, and for all Americans, and he appointed Bernard M. Baruch to plan the blueprint for reconversion of industry from war to peace.

He called on Congress for:

1. A realistic tax law which would tax all unreasonable profits, both individual and corporate.

2. Continuation of the renegotiation law.

3. A cost of food law to place a reasonable floor under farm prices and to place a ceiling on what the consumer has to pay.

4. Reenactment of the stabilization act.

5. A national service law to prevent strikes and draft labor for war jobs, if necessary.

It was on the first of these—the tax law— that the President ran into a Congressional revolt. Congressmen not only refused to raise an additional $10,000,000,000, limiting the bill to

$2,500,000,000, b...
over the Presid...
The Presiden...
the needy and...
On this point...
Barkley, of Ke...
fiery 45-minute...
impugning the...
But what app...
irretrievable br...
and Congress ou...
named unanim...
with Roosevelt.
Mr. Roosevel...
ing his return fr...
with the threat...
which would ha...
at the most cru...
also came the th...
The Chief Ex...
over the railro...
them over to...
incipient steel...
action, faded a...
back to their m...
He took a resi...
deep brown an...
the Democratic...
burning questio...
fourth term.
He told his...
Hannegan, of M...
Democratic Nat...
"I . . . will acc...
serve, if elected...
Hannegan h...
Democratic lead...
post, who had...
President when...
While he was...
blanca conferen...
nation of Edwa...
post of envoy t...
The appoint...
short but furiou...
Congress. It wa...
cans and Democ...
of paying off a...
One of the P...
returning from...
the Flynn nom...
Capitol Hill i...
so strong that...
the Senate.

tated, and Franklin Delano Roosevelt continued to function efficiently as before.

High had the distinction of being the only one whose departure from the inner council was announced officially. Most simply faded out of the picture, but the White House press secretary, Stephen Early, handed correspondents this statement:

"The President announced the death of the 'official spokesman' in March, 1933. [The White House spokesman was a Coolidge press-conference expedient.] He now announces the passing of the so-called authoritative spokesman—those who write as 'one of the President's close advisers.'"

The Saturday Evening Post in advertising an article by High had said: "Dr. High, who here, in a manner of speaking, reads the Democrats out of the Democratic party, has the Washington reputation of being one of the President's close advisers."

There were frequent criticisms of F.D.R.'s choice of men in whom to place confidence. One answer to that was that in Marshall, MacArthur, Eisenhower, King, Nimitz, he chose the right men to win the war. Other nations had to make repeated changes in their high commands; but the team Roosevelt chose after Pearl Harbor remained the winning team.

As President, Mr. Roosevelt loved to liken himself to the quarterback of the Nation's football team. Each play depended upon circumstances of the moment and those just gone by. He used to tell newspaper men he called signals on a trial-and-error basis and would cancel out his errors as quickly as he took advantage of his gains.

He was never discouraged by a setback. Many reforms which Congress rejected or the Supreme Court outlawed, he simply put back into law in only slightly modified form or accomplished by executive decree.

He liked making precedents. Like the time he, as President, wrote a letter directly to the Japanese emperor just because no one had ever addressed that dignitary through the mail.

Unlike the emperor, whose underlings believed he had been insulted when he was caricatured in an American magazine and made a formal protest to the State Department about it, the President never considered himself or his family above criticism. He naturally resented the adverse publicity given to his children about some of their doings, but he never reacted publicly.

The record of his sons after this country entered the war was a source of pride to Mr. Roosevelt. The eldest, James, became a lieutenant colonel of Marines, and was decorated for bravery. He fought at Midway, at the raid on Makin Island, on Guadalcanal and in the battles in the Central Pacific. Elliott rose to the rank of brigadier general in the Army Air Forces commanding a reconnaissance unit through the fighting in Tunisia, Sicily and Italy. Franklin Jr., a lieutenant on a destroyer, was decorated for bravery for services in the Mediterranean. The youngest son, John, whose bad eyesight disqualified him from combat duty, served with the Navy Supply Corps. The President's son-in-law, John Boettiger, became a lieutenant colonel in the Army who served abroad.

UNLIKE Wilson, who had waited until the end of the war to build machinery for the maintenance of peace, President Roosevelt started in 1944 to promote a permanent United Nations. At Dumbarton Oaks, near Washington, the groundwork was dug for it, and all the eligible nations were called to a meeting in San Francisco, in April 1945, to lay the foundations. Mindful of President Wilson's failure to gain approval of his peace treaty and League of Nations from the Congress, Mr. Roosevelt named a bi-partisan delegation to speak for the United States at San Francisco. He included Senator Tom Connally of Texas, chairman of the Senate Foreign Relations Committee, and Senator Arthur Vandenberg of Michigan, one of his most consistent critics.

In his last year, the Chief Executive had lived for two things and two things alone. They were victory over Germany and Japan, and a world peace structure that would last for generations to come.

The President's last year of life was a heart breaking struggle against time, a fact few persons realized fully.

The President's health first began to fail to a marked extent after his return from the Teheran conference in December of 1943. Influenza laid him low and he never fully recovered from it. A month's rest in South Carolina at Bernard M. Baruch's plantation estate restored him outwardly to health, but three grueling terms as President and the passage of years had taken their inexorable toll.

The fight over the Vice Presidential nomination at Chicago, which resulted in Harry S. Truman being chosen as a compromise candidate, indicated the degree of concern party chieftains held for the President's health.

He was plagued through his fourth term campaign by rumors that he was suffering from one malignant ailment after another and of a chronic heart ailment. It was true that he did undergo an operation in February, 1944, for removal of a "wen." His physicians watched his health zealously and countered all the rumors with an insistence that he was organically sound.

The President gave in, though reluctantly, to many of his physicians' demands. He dropped most of his luncheon conferences. For years he had carried his work right through his midday meals, snatching a light lunch in his office.

After lunch he usually would take a nap, returning to his work in the late afternoons. He slept later than usual in the mornings to gain more rest. But he drove himself relentlessly. He went to Pearl Harbor only a short time after his long winter's illness to hold the Pacific war conference with General Douglas MacArthur and Admiral Chester W. Nimitz that set the pattern for the reconquest of the Philippines and invasion of the Japanese home islands.

A short time after his return from there he headed for another conference at Quebec with Prime Minister Churchill.

Then he swung into a knockdown political campaign against the hard-swinging and youthful Governor of New York, Thomas E. Dewey. He insisted upon wearing ten-pound steel braces on his legs to enable him to stand up in a cold autumn rain at Ebbets Field, Brooklyn, and make a speech in behalf of the re-election of Sen. Wagner of New York, though every second was one of physical agony. The same day, though he suffered from a nagging sinus infection, he defiantly rode in an open car for four hours on a fifty-five mile swing about Metropolitan New York in a drenching downpour.

He repeated this at Philadelphia a week later in the campaign.

Not until several weeks after his re-election to a fourth term would he take a real rest. This time, in late November and early December, he went to Warm Springs. Fate was against him: he ran into three weeks of rainy, bitterly cold weather.

A short while later he took the oath of office for his fourth term on the south portico of the White House, bare-headed and top-coatless though a heavy snow was on the ground.

Then he headed for the Crimean conference where he sought to realize his main goal of setting the scene for the final victory over Germany and the meeting of the United Nations in San Francisco.

The conference sapped a great deal of his waning energies, for differences arose between the "Big Three" over the Polish question and other matters. Winston Churchill revealed later that he feared the President's health was ebbing at Yalta.

Some time after the conference closed, it was revealed that the United States would support a Russian demand for three seats in the assembly of the permanent United Nations organization.

The Polish settlement tentatively reached at Yalta also brought severe criticism in this country, especially when the Lublin regime delayed in reconstituting itself in accordance with the terms of the Crimea Declaration, and insisted with Russia's support on representation at San Francisco—a demand which Mr. Roosevelt rejected in one of his final diplomatic acts.

He rested on his two-week cruise by cruiser back to the States from Yalta—rested as much as his energies would permit. But wherever he went, by ship, train or plane, he was constantly in communication with Washington and the world's troubles.

When death came to him at Warm Springs he had just dictated the itinerary for his trip to the United Nations conference at San Francisco. Before many more weeks had passed, he again would have held another war and peace conference with Prime Minister Churchill.

And this time he had hoped that it would take him to Europe, with the war against Germany finally ended in crushing Allied victory. He hoped to go to London, to Paris and to Berlin.

FRANKLIN DELANO ROOSEVELT had a warmth of personality, a quick and ready tongue, sharp humor and the quality that our craft calls "a nose for news". That made him an unending source of not only dynamic "flash" stories, but those of warm color. Traveling with him about the world was like attending a five-ring circus, with ever-changing acts.

He was the first President to hold bi-weekly press conferences and to meet the spontaneous oral questions of the nation's press on every conceivable domestic and international subject. He answered those that he wished to readily; he parried others which he considered it impolitic to discuss at the moment, especially during the war, with trenchant humor.

The President liked to kid the men who wrote about him. When they questioned him about whether he would run for another term, he would tell them to put on the dunce cap and stand in the corner. He dodged penetrating questions by saying they were "iffy", and the correspondent should know better than asking them. But every now and then he would take a roundhouse swing at a reporter whose story had irked him. The special butts of his irony were columnists. He called one a "chronic liar."

To the three White House correspondents who traveled with him in wartime he spoke with the greatest frankness. Many of these talks "were off-the-record," and in these he told war plans, the peace he hoped to see made and the circumstances under which certain decisions had been made at Yalta or the other war conferences, and the reasons for them, with an oppenness that he could not maintain in his formal press conferences in Washington. These confidences were never broken by the newspapermen.

At Warm Springs, Georgia, where he frequently went to rest and swim in the natural warm waters, and where he died, he would stop the little open coupe that he drove around himself, by the roadside and hold informal conferences in the sun.

On the cruiser crossing the Atlantic on the way home from the Yalta conference a few weeks before his death we had lunch with him in the captain's quarters.

The President talked for nearly two hours. His conversation was engaging and covered a vast range of subjects. He spoke movingly when he dwelt upon the plans for making and securing a peace that would save the world from being plunged into another bloody war for generations to come.

He was a man whose visions took him centuries into the future. And these thoughts that he expressed were always of how to better the lot of mankind. He was particularly concerned about conservation of the nation's resources, and those of the world. His vast flood control, power and reforestation projects such as the Tennessee Valley Authority, and the similar ones he hoped would come into being for the Missouri, Ohio and Arkansas River valleys were to keep areas of

this country, a thousand years to come, from becoming desert areas as have much of Persia and other parts of the Middle East and North Africa.

He hoped to help Arabia, through the United Nations, restore water and fertility to the soil. He wanted to help bring education and a better mode of living to the millions of impoverished negroes in equatorial Africa.

He wanted to see peoples everywhere who may be held in bondage, educated, given greater opportunities for bettering themselves, and ultimately given their political freedom when they have demonstrated that they can govern themselves.

That controversy and debate should follow in the wake of his many actions, both in war and in peace, was only natural in a republic. His record of defying the founding fathers of the nation in accepting the Presidency for more than two terms—the only President ever to do this—and many other of his acts undoubtedly will be a matter for debate by the historians and future biographers of his life. He had an enormous power both to electrify and annoy. He never shrank from obstacles or enmities, and was not deterred from what he had his mind set on, by friends or enemies.

He once said, "I have always lost friends, but I have always had friends."

And, sweeping aside debate on the many controversial issues, he was conceded by both friends and enemies to be one of the most able leaders ever to emerge on the American scene. He may well be ranked as the outstanding man of his age in the world—an era which included the second World War and marked the turning point of the democratic form of government.

* * *

Radio and journalism made history on April 12, 1945, with their handling of one of the great stories of all time. The "inside" of the story is told in following excerpts from a report of William K. Hutchinson, manager of the Washington bureau of INS, and from a report by Columbia Broadcasting System. First, Hutchinson's:

At 5:45 p.m. Thursday, April 12, one of our trunk line wires showed an incoming call. Betsy Tupman, senior dictation typist, answered: "This is the INS." A male voice, speaking under some urgency, said: "Give me Mr. Slater quick. This is the White House." Mr. Slater, our day managing editor, had gone home, and Miss Tupman called to Erwin Sias, day news editor: "Get on 33 (the trunk line) quick. The White House is calling."

Sias answered and a woman, a White House telephone operator, asked, "INS?" and Sias replied, "Yes." The woman said, "Hold on."

A pause followed with Sias calling to Arthur Hermann, one of our roving correspondents who previously was day news editor, and to Arthur Hachten, night managing editor, to get on "33" as the White House was making a "conference call."

A "conference call" is the name given to the procedure when the White House telephones all three wire services, INS, AP and UP, and dictates a simultaneous release to them. The War Department does likewise. Some stories are important, some are not. There was no indication that this call was to be momentous. But the bureau was taking no chances, handling it just as though it would be a flash story.

With four of the INS staff on our phones, a White House male voice called out the roll. He called INS first and Sias answered, "INS here." Then he called the AP's name and a man replied; finally, the UP and a man replied. Then the White House male voice said, "Just a moment please."

Then came a new voice, rather faint, which said:

"This is Steve Early. I have a flash for you. The President died suddenly this afternoon."

Miss Tupman typed that out while Sias wrote it in longhand.

Instantly, Hermann and Hachten moved to the machines to send out the flash. For a final check, Hachten said quietly to Hermann, "FDR DEAD?" and Hermann nodded affirmatively. They flashed the death almost simultaneously. It came with the hand of our main office clock somewhere between 5:47 and 5:48 EWT, with the result that Charles Sparkenbaugh, night wire operator, timed his flash 5:47, while Milton Eglin, day wire operator, timed his 5:48.

By one of those mental quirks, both Hachten and Hermann shortened the written flash from "President died suddenly this afternoon" to "FDR dead." This may have been due psychologically to Hachten's whispered question.

Hermann then handled the first line of the sub flash on the day wire while Hachten was doing likewise on the night wire.

Miss Tupman meanwhile was taking Steve Early's announcement on carbons, one for dayside, one for nightside. There was an immediate and perhaps a natural interruption of Early by a girl from one of the other services, who inquired: "Do you mean President Roosevelt?"

And Early replied, rather irritated, "Yes, there's only one President."

A male voice then interrupted, asking: "Do you have a statement, Steve?"

To this Early replied: "No, I'm just giving you the facts. You're reporters. You write the story."

Then Early told of the President's death, believed to have been from a cerebral hemorrhage; that Mrs. Roosevelt had been notified; that she in turn had informed Vice President Truman; that Truman was at the White House and that Mrs. Roosevelt, Doctor McIntire and himself would go to Warm Springs that night.

When he was about finished, some one asked him: "What time did he die?" and Early replied: "I don't know—sometime early this afternoon." And at last Early said: "That's about all I have. You'll have to get the details from your reporters at Warm Springs."

Many other things happened almost simultaneously. Pierre Loving heard of the flash and left the State Department on his own volition to cross the street to the White House. Fred Tuttle was sent to the White House from the office.

As the flash went out, I was talking to Bill Theis, who was in the House gallery. Felix Cotten was dictating a story into the office from the Senate press gallery. Both were told immediately to get comment. Cotten told Neal, who was in the Senate gallery, too, and Neal left immediately for Truman's office in the Senate office building. Cotten began getting Senate comment.

Sias promptly phoned the Truman house and talked to his daughter Margaret. About five minutes elapsed before we cleared up Early's statement and then I sent Hermann to the White House and Sias took over the handling of the dayside story.

About 6:07 p.m. Bob Nixon finally got through on the telephone from Warm Springs and began dictating his on-the-scene story. We filed this immediately. A few minutes later we began to get from Loving, Tuttle and Hermann the statement given at the White House by Vice Admiral McIntire, the President's physician. We interrupted Nixon's file to put out McIntire's as it had some very dramatic details especially on how the White House itself found out the President first suffered a stroke, then lapsed into unconsciousness and finally died.

Bob Brown was writing Washington dateline leads for Hachten while I wrote one lead for the day wire. On the nightside Fenimore and Miss

McKee were getting up special articles while Miss Kearny and Marckres were getting up special items for both wires.

There was one question which we wanted answered. It was whether the San Francisco conference would be cancelled. So when the McIntire story was well on its way into the office I sent Loving back to the State Department to get that answer if possible from Stettinius.

The stories flowed smoothly meanwhile on both day and night wires. A dozen other staff members were given various assignments, all designed to give us a completely rounded story during the evening and for the early morning wire for Friday p.m. papers.

Cotten meanwhile left the Capitol and went to the White House. Cotten, Tuttle and Hermann set up a system for flashing Truman's inauguration. This was so effective that we actually flashed Truman taking his oath at 7:08 p.m., which was the moment of oath-taking.

The reporters who raced from the Truman ceremony to their telephones had arbitrarily agreed to date the oath-taking as having occurred at 7:09 p.m. We were unable to participate in that agreement because we had actually flashed a minute early.

At 7:15 p.m. Pierre Loving got the State Department announcement that the San Francisco conference would be held as scheduled. We put this out and cleared it at 7:19 p.m. It was routine from then on ...

From CBS' program log:

President Roosevelt's death came into the CBS newsroom at approximately 5:48 p.m. today.

First word was received on one of the International News Service wires and came direct from Washington. The ten bells on the teletype machine signifying news of great importance sent newswriter Lee Otis flying to the machine.

"I certainly wasn't expecting any such world-shattering report," he said later.

For there on the teletype were the words "bulletin"—and the shocking message. Otis turned and told his newsroom associates "the President is dead."

CBS news broadcasts director Paul White had already begun marshalling all the facilities and men at his command to cope with the tremendous and completely unexpected story. All regularly scheduled programs for the night were cancelled on CBS and broadcasts of eulogies and appropriate music substituted.

While news poured over the wires from the 13 news machines, including five United Press machines, three Associated Press wires, an OWI teletype, a Reuters British news machine and the ones that broke the story—the two International News Service machines, Peg Miller (Mrs. Paul White) who writes "Report to the Nation" began swiftly to gather biographical data for background material for the hastily improvised broadcasts.

All this time, the news was continually and regularly being sent over the air to CBS listeners by such men as major George Fielding Elliott, military and news authority; Ned Calmer, CBS foreign correspondent and reporter just returned from overseas and both CBS correspondents Bob Trout and John Daly who were most deeply shaken by the tragic and sudden death of the President.

Both Mr. Trout and Mr. Daly knew the President intimately and well and each had a deep affection for him personally. Said John Daly, "I had just strolled in to the news room to pick up my copy from the teletypes when I saw the news. It is the first time I have ever gone on the air reluctantly, to read to the people what I had before me."

* * *

This is how INS correspondents told the news of the passing of the President—these are documentary stories of a lasting interest comparable to the Ulster County Gazette's *account of the death of George Washington, and the* New York Herald's *dispatches relating to the death and funeral of Abraham Lincoln:*

By W. K. HUTCHINSON

WASHINGTON, Apr. 12—The White House announced this afternoon that President Roosevelt is dead.

The President died at Warm Springs, Ga.

President Roosevelt succumbed to a cerebral hemorrhage.

Mrs. Roosevelt was attending a meeting in Washington when the news reached the White House. Stephen Early, the President's secretary, telephoned to her. Early said: "When she came back, Admiral McIntyre and I went to her sitting-room and told her the President had slipped away.

"She was silent for a minute, and her first words were: 'I am more sorry for the people of this country and of the world than I am for us.'"

Vice President Harry S. Truman was informed of the President's death by Mrs. Roosevelt.

He rushed from the Capitol to the White House.

Members of the Cabinet also sped to the White House in response to a call for a Cabinet meeting. Secretary of State Edward R. Stettinius, Jr., had been informed earlier and was already at the White House. He hurried to Early's office from the State Department across the street, arriving at 5:40 P.M.

Mrs. Roosevelt meanwhile notified the four Roosevelt sons of their father's death in a message that said the President "slipped" away this afternoon.

Her message added that, "He did his job to the end as he would want you to do."

"Bless you all," Mrs. Roosevelt said to her sons, "And all our love." She signed the message "Mother."

Then the First Lady made preparations to leave Washington this afternoon with Vice Admiral Ross T. McIntire, the President's personal physician, and Early, for Warm Springs.

She announced that funeral services for the President will take place Saturday afternoon in the East Room of the White House and that the interment will be at Hyde Park Sunday.

Beyond that, Mrs. Roosevelt said, no detailed arrangements or exact times have been indicated.

By ROBERT G. NIXON

WARM SPRINGS, GA., April 12—President Roosevelt died suddenly this afternoon at his little white pine cottage atop Pine Mountain.

The great democratic leader's death came at 3:35 P.M., C.W.T. He died of a cerebral hemorrhage.

The President's death came without warning. He had been in Warm Springs for the last two weeks, getting in shape for his trip westward to greet the United Nations Conference at San Francisco.

He came to Warm Springs with a small staff of close associates to rest following his recent return from the strenuous Yalta conference.

The President's death was announced in mid-afternoon by Presidential Secretary William D. Hassett. Three White House correspondents of the press associations [INS, UP, AP] accompanying the President were summoned suddenly to the offices on the Warm Springs Foundation, near the "Little White House," and Hassett said to them:

"It is my sad duty to announce that the President died at 3:35 P.M. of cerebral hemorrhage."

With the President when he died was Commander Howard Bruenn of the Navy, who accompanied him to Warm Springs and who had been with him, together with Vice Admiral Ross T. McIntire, the President's personal physician, on many of his recent journeys, and Lieut. Comdr. George Fox, also of the Navy Medical Corps, and Dr. James Paullin. Also at the bedside were the President's secretary and close friend, William D. Hassett, and his personal secretary, Miss Grace Tully and two cousins, Miss Margaret Suckley and Miss Laura Delano, who had accompanied the President to Warm Springs.

The President left Washington without publicity a little over two weeks ago and went to Hyde Park. He was there for a few days before returning to Washington for less than a day, when he resumed his journey southward to the Georgia resort where he had spent many weeks during the years in which he was head of the nation.

During his stay here the President had enjoyed a period of perfect weather. He had taken long drives in the green-leafed countryside about the Foundation. He was tanned a ruddy brown. He appeared to be in good health up to a few moments before he said, "I have a terrible headache"—his last words.

Mr. Roosevelt apparently said that as he recovered momentarily from the faint that had caused doctors to be called to his side.

Commander Bruenn said: "The President was in excellent spirits this morning. I saw him at 9:30."

A batch of bills and other documents were brought to the President shortly after noon by his secretary, William D. Hassett. The documents had arrived later than usual, as the plane in which they were being flown was grounded enroute and then the train bringing the pouch to Warm Springs was tied up behind a freight wreck.

Because of the lateness of the arrival of the pouch, and it being near the President's lunchtime, Hassett asked him whether he wanted to do his signature work then or later in the afternoon. The President replied: "I'll do it now, Bill." As the President signed the various papers, including the Commodity Credit Corporation bill, using a small table placed in front of the big stone fireplace, he looked up at Hassett, and his face brought into one of his characteristic broad smiles. As was his custom, Hassett said, as he

eme": President

s indicated by

had been ar-
ew close associ-
made over the
Georgia. The
cottage of the
Allcorn, atop
President's cot-

planned to at-
in the main
Foundation by
to have made a
inners by radio.
last night.

ompanying the
together with
esident's arriv-
suddenly to the
Secretary Has-

Springs the
the affairs of
so heavily. He
rgio Osmena of
Osmena, who
Manila, that he
independence by
the date when
assure is sched-

that the Amer-
full value the
American troops
against the Jap-

correspondents
itting and work
sident said that
take broad steps
horrors of war
blame for the
by the war.
to replace the
ies and build-
in the war.
warfare against
nally stripped
military men-

The President declared that the mandated islands which were given to Japan after the last world war must be taken from them.

Japan, he asserted, must be prevented, as the Germans must be, from any possible aggression in the world again. Japan's main bases in the Pacific and on the continent of Asia, he continued, must also be taken from them. His own words were that Japan must after the war be policed both internally and externally.

The President said he and Osmena had talked about what bases the United States must take over to secure the Pacific from further Japanese aggression in the foreseeable future. The Philippines, he said, will be an important part of the future security bases.

The Chief Executive said that he expected organized Japanese resistance in the Philippines to be ended by Autumn when he planned to grant the Philippines their independence.

Asked who would administer the mandated islands taken from the Japanese, the President said that that would be done by the United Nations. But he made it crystal clear that the United States must have a large, if not complete part, in assuring the future security of the Pacific areas.

Treasury Secretary Henry Morgenthau was President Roosevelt's last official visitor. Morganthau dined with the President Wednesday night. He stopped at Warm Springs enroute back to Washington from Daytona Beach, Fla., where he had been visiting his wife who is convalescing from an illness.

Aside from Morgenthau and President Osmena of the Philippines, the President had no other official visitors during his two-weeks' rest here.

The story of the latter's visit was ordered held until our return to Washington in order to preserve the secrecy surrounding the President's travels.

Mr. Roosevelt had planned to be back at the White House in Washington on Friday, April 20 to greet the regent of Iraq. He then intended to make a brief visit to Hyde Park before proceeding to the United Nations Conference at San Francisco, which he was scheduled to open on April 25.

Instead a funeral train will leave warm Springs tomorrow for Washington, where it will arrive Saturday morning.

Tonight the President lay in simple dignity in a plain maple bed in his unpretentious bedroom overlooking the broad pine-filled Georgia Valley to which he had first come 20 years ago to recu-perate from the after effects of infantile paralysis. In addition to the single bed, the room contained a mahogany, leather-topped desk; a maple chest of drawers, table and reading lamp and scatter hook-rugs on the floor. The walls were adorned with ship prints and a ship's barometer, reminiscent of the sea life the President loved.

Outside the white pine cottage, Marines and the Secret Service detail that protected the President in life, maintained a vigil tonight.

By DAMON RUNYON

Damon Runyon has written many great stories for International News Service that will live as shining examples of creative American journalism, but the story that follows is more than just another example. It is Runyon at his best; it is Runyon with his sensitive feeling for human beings and their emotions, woven with a masterful touch into the running news story of an historic funeral cortege. Yet it is a story told simply and with the restraints of a truly great craftsman.

WASHINGTON, April 14.—The funeral cortege of the late President Roosevelt, a comparatively small, war-begrimed cavalcade, passed through the streets of Washington this morning from the railroad station to the White House, where simple religious services were held this afternoon before the body was taken to his old home in Hyde Park for burial tomorrow.

The procession was the only touch of military pomp to the funeral of the dead chieftain of the mightiest armed force on the face of the earth.

Hundreds of thousands of the people of Washington packed the sidewalks along Constitution and Pennsylvania Avenues, and watched the passing of the mournful troop.

At the corner of 12th Street and Constitution Avenue stood a well-dressed, confident appearing man, a prosperous business man, perhaps, with a boy in his mid-teens but tall for his years. He could look over the heads of most of those wedged in 10-deep ahead of him.

"I remember his smile, father," the boy was saying. "I mean I remember it from the pictures of him in the newsreels. It was such a wonderful smile. It crinkled his face up all around his eyes."

"Yes, he smiled a lot," the man said. "I used to say he smiled to think of the way he had fellows like me over a barrel. I hated him.

"I hated him most of the 12 years he lived in

this town. I mean I hated him politically. Now I wonder why. He only did the best he could. No man could do more."

Against a sky of crystal, flocks of silvery planes roared overhead at intervals, gleaming in the sunlight. But when the noise of their motors had died away the whole city seemed strangely quiet.

The shrill whistles of the traffic policemen, the clip-clop of feet hurrying over the pavements and the low hum of human voices were the only sounds and they carried far in the eerie silence.

It was as if by signal everyone had said "Let us all be very quiet," and the whole community fell into restrained mood as it awaited the passing of the funeral party this morning.

Yet one knew that at this very moment, across two oceans, the American guns this man who lies dead had mobilized were bombing what was at once the thunder of his triumph and the vast volleys for those who died in the service of their country, as he had undoubtedly died.

"He wore funny hats, father," the boy said. "I remember the one he had on when he was in North Africa to see the soldiers, and he was riding in a jeep. He turned his hat up in the front and back. He wore funny hats when he went fishing, too."

"Yes, and I used to think his head was too big for them—for any hat," the man said. "I know now that was a foolish idea. Why should he have been swell headed—a great man like him? What crazy things I said about him!"

It was hot. Sweat ran down the faces of the steel-helmeted soldiers standing along the street in heavy flannel shirts. These were no parade troops. They wore crumpled looking uniforms, they looked field stained.

A man, coatless and bareheaded, carrying a sleepy-looking child in his arms, held the youngster up so it could see over the heads of the crowd and softly said, "Look, look."

Some day that child may be telling its grandchildren that she saw the funeral of President Roosevelt as grandparents used to tell of seeing the funeral of President Lincoln.

Mothers leading children by the hands instructed them to wiggle in between the close packed spectators to the front lines. No one complained about the children.

Everyone talked in a low voice. There was an impatient turning of heads as some people setting up empty boxes on which to stand chattered loudly for a moment, their voices disturbing the funeral hush.

Small boys perched in the trees along the avenue now green in the early Spring.

Footloose soldiers and sailors including officers wandered through the crowd. Canadian service girls in their spic and span uniforms and king black stockings stepped smartly along the street.

Heads showed in clusters at every window in the low temporary war buildings and on the steps and in every jutting place on the solemn looking government buildings that would afford a foothold.

Tradesmen wearing aprons and artisans wearing overalls pressed against the police lines.

Now the tump of drums, at first faint and far-off, but quickly getting stronger, broke the silence and then came the wail of a funeral march played by a band, and an auto loaded with officers passed, then a squad of motorcycle policemen on their machines. The street signals on the avenue kept changing to "stop" and "go" all through the procession.

The people stood with their arms folded, those in back of the first row teetering on their tiptoes trying to get at least a fleeting glimpse of the procession.

The Marine band, the musicians in white caps and blue uniforms, their great silver horns flashing, footed it along to the slow strains of the funeral music.

"They say he always had to wear a terrible steel brace like poor little Jackie Clark and like Cousin Nellie, too," the boy said. "They say he suffered greatly just as they do. Is that true, father? He must have been very brave."

"Yes," the man said, "he suffered greatly. I read once he fought all the better because he fought in chains. He was a game man. That I always said. A very game man. No man could be gamer."

Now came a battalion from Annapolis, the cadet officers with drawn swords, the cadets in blue uniforms with white caps and white leggings and guns slanted across their shoulders.

Then a battalion of field artillery, the soldiers sitting stiffly upright on their gun carriers which moves four abreast, the engines throttled down so that they made scarcely any noise.

Used-looking field pieces painted a dingy red were towed behind trucks loaded with their crews, and the faces of all these soldiers seemed absolutely expressionless under their helmets.

"I remember so many little things about him, father," said the boy. "I remember his nose-glasses. I often wondered how he kept them on his nose, even when he was out in a storm. He never seemed to mind what kind of weather it was."

"Yes," the man said, "I guess all the people will remember little things about him in the years to come. I once said that when it came to weather he didn't mind hell or high water if he had to put one of his ideas across. But it was a snide remark. I made too many snide remarks about him in his lifetime."

Another band, some colored artillerymen marching on foot, then a band of sailor musicians, their dolorous march music throbbing on the still air.

A battalion of bluejackets and then a battalion of women's armed force units, the Wacs and Waves and women Marines marching rather loosely in the absence of quickstep music.

Movie cameramen on trucks weaved along the line of march. The crowd watched in silence.

And now at last came the flag-swathed casket on an artillery caisson drawn by six strapping big gray horses in brightly polished harness, four of them mounted by soldiers.

The President's flags were borne just behind the caisson and then came the automobiles loaded with the great men of the nation.

But with the passing of the casket, the crowd began breaking up, still strangely silent. They had seen the funeral cortege of a fellow citizen, who in other nations and other times would have had the death panoply of a Caesar but who, as it was, probably had more than he would have wished.

"I remember when he got his little dog Fala," the boy said. "I think they must have loved each other a great deal, father, as much as my Mugs and I love each other. You could tell it in the newsreels when they were together. I think he must have been a very kind man to be so nice to a little dog. I hope they take good care of Fala."

"Yes," the man said, "he was a kind man. He was kind to many people. I used to say I hated him when he was alive but now it is difficult for me to pick out any one reason why. How could I hate a kind man?"

By INEZ ROBB

HYDE PARK, N. Y., April 15.—The inconsolable sobs of a little child, frightened beyond understanding by the awful solemnity of the burial of a President, echoed sharply today through a garden bright with spring sun.

They drowned out the muffled weeping of men and women as the mortal remains of Franklin Delano Roosevelt were committed to the beloved earth of his ancestral home.

As the U. S. Military Academy band softly played *Nearer My God to Thee* and then, triumphantly, *The Star Spangled Banner,* the little black dog Fala rolled in the grass at the feet of Miss Margaret Suckley, who held his leash.

But the hush that held the mourners in thrall as the music stopped and the committal service began, affected even the dog, who sat quietly, looking from time to time at the bowed figure of the gray faced woman, Mrs. Franklin Delano Roosevelt, only a few feet away.

When the first of three volleys from the rifles of a West Point firing squad echoed over the President's grave, the little dog jumped to his feet and barked sharply—as in protest at something he sensed but could not understand.

All over the beautiful garden, just beginning to burgeon with spring, there was soft sobbing, the only sound as the volleys echoed away.

In front of the grave, Brigadier General Elliott Roosevelt, who flew home from England to attend his father's funeral, wiped the moisture from his eyes with a shaking fist.

But the iron control of the widowed Eleanor Roosevelt never faltered as she stood between her only daughter, Mrs. Anna Roosevelt Boettiger, and the only one of her four sons, all in the armed services, who could reach home in time for their father's funeral.

A few paces in the rear, her four pretty young daughters-in-law, clad in black from head to toe as was their mother-in-law and sister-in-law, struggled to emulate her.

But with difficulty and without much success. The tears would come, and there was nothing they could do about them.

A few paces in the rear of the family stood the thirty-second President of the United States, Harry S. Truman, Chief Executive by grace of the death of this man now being laid to final rest.

The new President did not weep. But his jaws were clenched until the muscles stood out in a determined effort at self-control.

His eyes blinked behind his horn-rimmed glasses as he bowed his head to repeat, in unison with the throng, the Lord's Prayer.

Mrs. Truman, in gray, and their daughter, Margaret had even more difficulty than the President in preserving the outward signs of self-control.

Toward the end of this solemn service, an

Army sergeant with seven hash marks on his sleeve, walked the few paces from the grave to Mrs. Roosevelt, saluted and presented her with the flag which had covered the President's bier during the trip from Warm Springs, through the funeral procession and ceremony in Washington yesterday, and finally on the journey to Hyde Park and the sunny garden in Krum Elbow.

Mrs. Roosevelt, with a smile summoned from some source of inner strength, leaned forward to accept it and said, "Thank you."

For a split second, the sergeant looked at her with mingled amazement and respect. In the next instant, he whipped off his cap and bowed low before this woman who has made history no less than her husband.

Only once, at the end of the service as she turned to leave the garden, did it seem that Mrs. Roosevelt's control would at last snap. As she started, she noticed a few feet away a very old lady who had been helped into the garden and who had sat, a gray rug over her knees, throughout the ceremony.

She walked at once to Mrs. James Roosevelt, the widow of President Roosevelt's long dead half-brother, who is buried at Hyde Park in the family plot beyond St. James Church where Roosevelts have worshipped for generations. Mrs. Roosevelt kissed the old woman and then the President's cousins, Miss Suckley and Mrs. Laura Delano. Only then, as she turned to join her son and daughter, did her face begin to work and her shoulders drop.

Instantly, Mrs. Roosevelt stopped short. In a matter of seconds she squared her black-clad shoulders. She lifted her head with resolution and walked out of the garden. . . .

By ROBERT G. NIXON

HYDE PARK, N. Y., April 15.—Franklin Delano Roosevelt was buried today with all the military pomp and ceremony befitting the Commander-in-Chief of the mightiest nation.

The grave was dug in the lawn of the rose garden just east of the President's field-stone ancestral manor house.

Walling in the 150-foot square garden is a cedar hedge 15 feet high. The grave is in the center and south side of the garden.

On all sides of the square, their backs to the hedge, battle veterans of the fields of strife in Europe and the Pacific stood rigidly at attention.

In a group on the right were the nation's great into whose hands, with President Truman, has now fallen the conduct of the war and the realization of their dead leader's dream of world peace for generations to come.

A little group of Hyde Park villagers stood behind the flower-laden bier.

The President's body was brought back to his Hudson Valley home on a funeral train that moved through the night from Washington.

Tens upon thousands stood beside the stations in the towns and cities during the night to view the lighted funeral car.

The funeral cortege began its march at 10 a.m. of a sunlit Sabbath morn. The muffled beat of drums heralded its approach to where the friends of the President stood waiting beside the grave.

The cortege was headed by the West Point band. Then came the battalion of cadets led by officers with drawn sabers marching in threes through lanes of soldiers, sailors and marines in slow funeral cadence to the mournful beat of the drums, muffled in black crepe, and the strains of Chopin's *Funeral March*.

The black artillery caisson, drawn by seven brown horses, bearing the flag-covered casket, followed.

Behind came the black-draped steed, symbol of the warrior fallen, led by a colored trooper.

The family followed in two black cars.

At 10:35 the band began *Hail to the Chief*, the march of welcome to President Roosevelt throughout his long period of service to the nation, then swept into the strains of the *Star Spangled Banner*.

Moments later the flag-draped casket was borne into the garden through an archway in the cedar hedge.

As the body was lowered into the grave the Rev. W. George Anthony, white-haired 78-year-old rector of St. James Episcopal, the President's church in which he served as senior warden, intoned:

"Now the laborer's task is o'er; now the battle day is past . . .

"Father, in Thy gracious keeping, leave us now our brother sleeping."

A child wailed.

The rifle squad slanted their muskets into the air. There was a muffled drum beat. Three volleys cracked.

The casket sank into the grave. Franklin Roosevelt was home again; home for the ages.